THE METAPHYSICAL BOOK OF
GEMS
AND
CRYSTALS

THE METAPHYSICAL BOOK OF
GEMS
AND
CRYSTALS

FLORENCE MÉGEMONT

TRANSLATED BY JUDITH ORINGER

Healing Arts Press
Rochester, Vermont

Healing Arts Press
One Park Street
Rochester, Vermont 05767
www.HealingArtsPress.com

Healing Arts Press is a division of Inner Traditions International

Originally published in French under the title *Dictionnaire des pierres et minéraux* by
   Éditions Exclusif
First U.S. edition published in 2008 by Healing Arts Press

Note to the reader: *This book is intended as an informational guide. The remedies, approaches,
and techniques described herein are meant to supplement, and not to be a substitute for, professional medical care or treatment. They should not be used to treat a serious ailment without prior
consultation with a qualified health care professional.*

LIBRARY OF CONGRESS CATALOGING-IN-PUBLICATION DATA

Mégemont, Florence.
   [Dictionnaire des pierres et minéraux. English]
   The metaphysical book of gems and crystals / Florence Mégemont ; translated by Judith
Oringer.
      p. cm.
   Summary: "Details the powerful effects of gems as an alternative therapy for physical,
psychological, and spiritual healing"—Provided by publisher.
   ISBN-13: 978-1-59477-214-6 (pbk.)
   ISBN-10: 1-59477-214-2 (pbk.)
   1. Gems—Miscellanea. 2. Precious stones—Miscellanea. 3. Crystals—Miscellanea. 4.
Occultism. 5. Healing. 6. Spiritual healing. I. Title.
   BF1442.P74M4413 2008
   133'.25538—dc22

                                                                    2007028666

Printed and bound in the United States by Versa Press, Inc.

10 9 8 7 6

Text design by Jon Desautels and layout by Virginia Scott Bowman
This book was typeset in Garamond Premier Pro with Gill Sans and Trajan as display typefaces

Chapter 5 chakra art from *The Chakras in Shamanic Practice* by Susan J. Wright, courtesy of
Destiny Books, Rochester, Vermont.

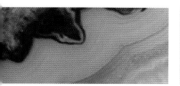  

CONTENTS

--------------- PART 1 ---------------
WORKING WITH GEMSTONES

Agate • Alabaster • Amazonite • Amber • Amethyst • Ametrine •
Andalusite • Aquamarine • Aragonite • Aventurine • Azurite •
Beryl • Calcite • Carnelian • Celestine • Chalcedony • Chrysoberyl •
Chrysocolla • Chrysolite • Chrysoprase • Citrine • Coral •
Crystal: Cathedral Crystal, Herkimer Crystal, Phantom Crystal,
Rainbow Crystal, Rock Crystal, Scepter Crystal • Diamond •
Emerald • Fluorite • Garnet • Gem Salt • Heliotrope • Hematite •
Iolite • Jade • Jasper • Jet • Kunzite • Labradorite • Lapis Lazuli •
Magnesite • Magnetite • Malachite • Meerschaum • Mica •
Moldavite • Moonstone • Nephrite • Obsidian • Olivine • Onyx •
Opal • Orpiment • Pearl • Peridot • Pyrite • Rhodochrosite •
Rhodonite • Rose Quartz • Ruby • Sapphire • Silicified Wood •
Smoky Quartz • Sodalite • Sulfur • Sunstone • Tanzanite •
Tiger's Eye • Topaz • Tourmaline • Turquoise • Zirconium

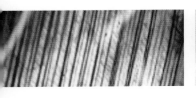  

PART 2

GEMSTONE CORRESPONDENCES WITH THE CHAKRAS, COLORS, AND SIGNS OF THE ZODIAC

PART 3

TREATMENT FOR SPECIFIC CONDITIONS

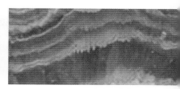

INTRODUCTION

THE THERAPEUTIC USE OF GEMS AND CRYSTALS

Stones have been used for therapeutic purposes since the beginning of time. Sorcerers and magicians, the "magical" men of the earliest communities, communed with the mineral world and used stones to heal a variety of illnesses. It was believed that stones came from heaven and remained alive after their "fall."

Some believed they contained a particle of the divine breath, while others imagined that an animal, snake, or toad lived inside even the smallest pebble. It was also believed that each stone retained the heat it received from the sun.

In ancient China, the Manchurians considered stones to be the tree's sister. To them, stones represented static energy as opposed to the cycle of vegetal growth. Stones, the unchanging principle of integral life, were thus able to restore all human faculties.

This permanent symbol of life also represented the triumph of life over death. Stones still mark the final resting place of our loved ones— we go to the stone to celebrate and remember the life of the person. There is also the widespread custom of throwing or placing stones on a tomb, or of burying the deceased with one or several precious stones. The tombs of the poor were often topped with only a simple stone engraved with a magical sign. In contrast, the royal tombs in Egypt were studded with precious jade and lapis lazuli. The ancients' knowledge of the power of minerals suggests that the use of these stones ran much deeper than mere aesthetics.

THE ANCESTORS OF LITHOTHERAPY

In Asia, jade and jasper, are revered as noble stones. In the past, the medicinal use of these stones was subject to strict laws and breaking a jade object was immediately punished with death.

Jade, believed to be charged with yang energy, was accorded solar qualities. It was believed to be a panacea, the remedy for all diseases. According to the Chinese alchemist Ko-hung, it was thought that gold and jade, placed in the nine openings of the deceased, would keep the cadaver from putrefying. Placing pearls, said to contain yin energy, in the burial place ensured rebirth and reincarnation.

Witch doctors gave certain stones to sick people who rubbed them over the affected part of their bodies. The stone was believed to absorb the disease. Afterward, no one was allowed to touch the stone, since it was thought they could contract the disease contained in the mineral.

During the medieval period, building stones also served as medicine: the powder obtained by scratching the walls of a church was known to cure many illnesses.

Some stones were also used to concoct poisons. During the Renaissance, the Borgias used poison to eliminate their powerful rivals. This led to a curious confusion: it was thought that this murderous family's favorite poison contained nail clippings. In reality, Borgias' poison contained onyx powder (*onyx* means "nail" in Greek), which, when accompanied by the powder of other minerals, can become toxic.

The importance of the black stone in Mecca illustrates the importance of minerals in that civilization. This fifty-foot stone stands in the center court of the Great Mosque. Forgiveness of sin is guaranteed to all who touch it.

Precious stones, from north Africa to Arabia, were charged with precise symbolism and believed to create magical powers. Wearing turquoise ensured victory, while carnelian and amber offered protection from the evil eye. The translucent stones were thought to be especially powerful. They were believed to contain the power of water in crystallized form, and this concentrated force was often used for magical and divinatory purposes. Wise men and fortune-tellers all made use of these stones.

In Greece and Rome, stones were used for counting. Small stones were worth one unit; others, five or ten units—as with the Chinese abacus. This made it possible to make a list of the herds, evaluate merchandise, and inventory goods. In Latin, a pebble was called calculus or *scrupulus*. The word *calculate* has stayed with us and is still used in a mathematical context. These commercial practices led to speculation about the symbolic meanings of numbers. Stones were used in this debate, which eventually led to the esoteric practice of numerology.

The ancient Mexicans made hatchets and knives out of polished stone. These instruments of death, serving in human sacrifices, also represented rebirth, the cycle of the seasons—even eternity. These sacred tools were often made out of jade or obsidian, two stones that have great symbolic meaning.

In the Celtic tradition, stones were associated with fertility. Women in Brittany would scratch the tablets of the dolmens—megalithic monuments consisting of a large, flat stone laid horizontally across upright stones—and rub their bellies with the stone powder to become fertile. Granite, with its slight radioactivity, is conducive to pregnancy.

STONES AND RELIGIOUS TRADITIONS

In the Judeo-Christian tradition stones symbolized wisdom and permanence. They quenched the mystical thirst, just as water satisfies the body's thirst. Traces of this symbolism can be found in the story of Moses who, when entering and leaving the desert, strikes a stone with his stick to create a stream of water. The "philosopher's stone," referring to the gospels, was also called "the Lord's bread." The angular stone has many, apparently contradictory, esoteric meanings.

Stones that are nurturing are another biblical theme: the devil tempts Christ by asking him to change stones into bread. Christ changed the name of a fisherman, calling him Peter (Pierre in French, which means stone) and "on this stone" founded the Church. Man, who is perishable and mortal, would become the first stone of a mystical edifice that has survived for two thousand years.

Precious stones in the Judeo-Christian tradition also represent transmutation, the sister of transfiguration. We move from the opaque to the transparent in the course of our evolutionary journey.

The German mystic Hildegard of Bingen wrote one of the first treatises on mineralogy that included the therapeutic qualities of each mineral. During the building of the great cathedrals in Europe, an extremely rich symbolism of the stones was developed. It was the era of the "stone masters," the original freemasons. These builders were said to have passed along esoteric secrets to the less educated laborers as they traveled from site to site.

The city walls of the new Jerusalem were built in jasper and enhanced with various stones. The first stratum was jasper; the second, sapphire; the third, chalcedony; the fourth, emerald; the fifth, sardonyx; the sixth, carnelian; the seventh, chrysolite; the eighth, beryl; the ninth, topaz; the tenth, chrysoprase; the eleventh, hyacinth; the twelfth, amethyst. The twelve gates of the city were said to be twelve delicate pearls.

It was not just a question of beauty or munificence; the symbolism of each stone was believed to be beneficial to the city.

THE BASIC VIBRATORY PATTERN

The intuitions of the ancients regarding stones are confirmed by modern science. The basic vibratory pattern, which controls the color and sound spectrum (the same word, *chromatic*, is used in both cases), is found in all physical phenomena, from electromagnetic waves to ripples in the water, or the infinite movement of electrons.

The apparent inertia of the smallest pebble shouldn't fool us; each pebble is both a transmitter and a receiver of various vibrations. Each stone vibrates and emits its own unique radiance. This radiance interacts with the electromagnetic field of our bodies in ways that still remain mysterious.

The great assemblage of megaliths at Carnac (in Brittany, France) and Stonehenge (England), and the obelisks and pyramids of Egypt and of pre-Columbian America, can all be thought of as wave receivers. These monuments captured cosmic energy and redistributed it to the ground. The stones, believed to be connected to the planets, had not yet revealed all their secrets to the ancients, but people did note strange phenomena associated with them. In fact, we only know a little bit more about them today; the stones still have many secrets to reveal.

THE ANCIENT ART OF LITHOTHERAPY: HEALING WITH STONES

Throughout recorded history, scholars, magicians, alchemists, and doctors have studied the stones with inexhaustible patience. Some spent their lives at it, and centuries passed before the effects of some stones were established with certainty. This slow transmission, this thousand-year-old journey, is the basis of modern lithotherapy.

Many interesting discoveries were made along the way. A king who was subject to epilepsy, abrupt attacks of anger that were dangerous for the country, or digestive problems that made him spiteful or cruel would turn into a wise and skillful politician as soon as he wore a crown or a pectoral ornamented with diamonds. Scholars noted this fact and used the diamond's intrinsic property to cure others with the same problems.

Since not everyone was a king, efforts were made, using the quality of the colors, to find less costly stones with similar effects. It was found that rock crystal could be used in place of diamonds to heal some illnesses. In the same way, a peasant woman suffering from menstrual problems could be healed with coral, malachite, or chrysocolla, while the queen was treated with rubies for the same problem. The stone's purity is part of the equation. Rubies transmit more energy than the less costly stones, and the queen healed more quickly. Nevertheless, the peasant women still saw their pains and irregularity disappear. In ancient China and Egypt, the poor were allowed to rent or borrow stones when needed for lithotherapy.

LITHOTHERAPY AND MODERN MEDICINE

Today, lithotherapy is a safe alternative to overprescribed pharmaceuticals. Repeated throat problems, for example, don't always need to be treated with antibiotics. An amber, tourmaline, topaz, or chalcedony stone worn as a pendant can be just as effective. Cortisone is often prescribed for skin diseases. Aventurine, sapphire, or rock crystal can also treat these problems without the frightening side effects of that drug. This radiance of the mineral world is similar to electrotherapy or radiology—but without the potential dangers. There is not much risk with stones used externally. The most that might happen is a slight fever or a bit of vertigo, if you have too much contact with a powerful stone.

Practicing lithotherapy does not mean that we turn our backs on the extraordinary accomplishments of modern medicine. Antibiotics, when not overused, can be effective, and vaccines have saved the lives of millions of people.

Lithotherapy can be used to treat many types of ailments but it cannot cure everything. Some serious illnesses and infections require more invasive medical treatment. If this is the case, lithotherapy can be used to mitigate any harmful side effects. For example, this kind of therapy will work wonders for postoperative shock. Although lithotherapy can't heal psychoses—modern medicine cannot heal it either—it can help to soothe those who suffer from these illnesses.

Some stones, such as calcium and magnesium, have pharmaceutical qualities. This is the effective principle of mineral waters and many medicinal preparations. Compounded lithium, a mineral element, is used for serious mental disturbances. Silica, among other minerals, is included in the basic substances used in homeopathic drugs. In the past, various infections were cured by absorbing powdered stones. Even so, some of the remedies could have been more harmful than the disease. Orpiment, for example, was long considered a panacea. Although it was able to alleviate some pains momentarily, it is nonetheless a source of arsenic, and its effects can be fatal over time. Likewise, you will not heal anything by ingesting calcite or limestone: the dosage, grinding, and dissolving are factors that only professionals know how to control. Instructions for making stone waters are given in this book for some of the safer stones. (See Stone Waters and Elixirs in chapter 2.) However, it is always best to consult a trained medical professional before ingesting any stone preparation.

MEDITATION AND LITHOTHERAPY

Lithotherapy is not just a type of medicine. In addition to their curative applications, stones can also help to strengthen us mentally, emotionally, and spiritually. Wearing a particular stone can have a regenerative effect. But meditating on a particular stone is an even more active way of balancing our inner energies. We can start by looking, touching, and playing with a particular stone. We can connect even more deeply by meditating on its beauty, origins, qualities, and symbolism. There are many different meditation techniques—Zen, Hindu, and Christian contemplation—that can connect us with the telluric, primeval force of each mineral.

STONES AND INDIGENOUS CULTURES

Women in India and the aborigines of southern Australia absorb the dust from the monolithic representations of lingua (a stone statue representing a male sexual organ) to become fertile. The Fang, a tribal group in the west African country of Gabon, place granite between the legs of a laboring woman to aid in childbirth. The women of the Yakout, an aboriginal ethnic group in eastern Siberia, drink stone water made from a similar stone before giving birth.

In the Cordillera mountain chain of the Andes, in Chile and Peru, and in Tibet and Siberia, piles of various stones are found at crossroads and at the entrance to mountain passes; every traveler adds to the pile. These stones are said to bear a bit of the soul of each traveler. The fragments of these individual souls will create a powerful, collective "mineral soul" to protect travelers from the hazards of the road.

Stones in Africa are used to gather the energy of the souls of the dead. These stones can protect people from thunder or provoke misfortune in those who have offended or defiled them. In this area, stones are also believed to be symbols of fertility.

In Mongolia, shamans range continuously across the mountains and plains, trying to find a stone with magical climatic properties in the belly of a steer or the head of stag. These stones are said to have the power to bring wind, rain, ice, and snow to their enemies and are also used to control the severity of the seasons.

To experience the mysterious power of the stones for yourself, all you have to do is relax, touch a stone, and allow yourself be overtaken by its energy. When you do, you will be convinced of the powerful effects of this radiance.

This guidebook is not meant to be a substitute for the medical advice of an experienced lithotherapist. However, it will introduce you to the stones and explain their many uses. I invite you to delve into the world of lithotherapy by discovering and appreciating the gems and crystals presented here.

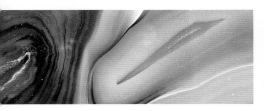 

PART ONE

Working with Gemstones

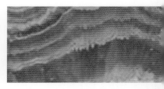

1
DIRECTORY OF GEMS AND CRYSTALS

Seventy-four gems and crystals are featured in this chapter. Arranged alphabetically—from agate to zirconium—each description includes the stone's chemical composition, colors, areas of principal deposits, and hardness and density ratings. The hardness ratings are based on the Mohs' scale and the density, measured as grams per cubic centimeter, is equal to the stone's specific gravity. Extended information about the etymology of each stone's name as well as the stone's general characteristics, therapeutic uses, and zodiac correspondences is also presented. This informative text is accompanied by photographs of the gems and crystals, providing a comprehensive introduction to each stone's particular characteristics and healing qualities.

AGATE

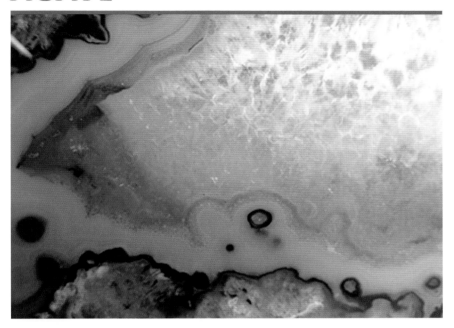

Chemical composition: Silicon dioxide

Color: Blue, yellow, black, crimson, and green. It is also colorless.
Note: Some agates are artificially colored. The particular qualities of
the different colors are discussed below.

Principal deposits: Germany, Italy, the Americas (Brazil, Uruguay,
Mexico, Texas), and India

Hardness: 6.5 to 7

Density: 2.5

Etymology and General Characteristics

According to the ancient philosopher Pliny the Elder, Agate is the
name of a Sicilian river in the region of Sélinonte where this stone
is found. The name of the river, like the name of the stone, evokes a
Greek word meaning that which is beautiful and good.

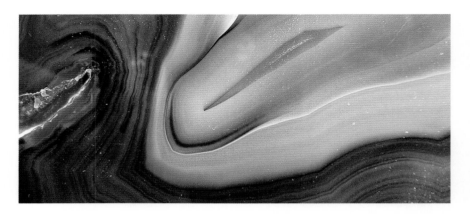

This stone is part of the quartz group, a variety of chalcedony delicately laid down in concentric layers. Agate is found in various forms: lined, milky, arborized, herborized (moss agate), or banded according to the arrangement of colors. Agate has many colors and each color is associated with unique meanings.

Blue agate: Dear to the French poet Francis Jammes, its color evokes the "April skies." Yet this is also one of the most earthly stones. Its color evokes a complementary sense of balance.

Yellow agate: When mixed with crystalline traces, it evokes gold and wealth, from the material point of view. This is why a great many traditions believe it has the power to help discover hidden treasures. From the spiritual point of view, gold represents both faithful friendship and burning desire. An agate that is mostly yellow is thought to be a stone of seduction and good for men who want to attract women. It can also cause us to long for wealth and spiritual powers.

Black agate (and its varieties—sardonyx, carnelian, and onyx): These stones enhance the inner life and meditation. They act as a mirror enabling us to contemplate and go within. Black agate is the stone of the spiritual quest, the one that Theseus, the legendary king of Athens, found in the sea and offered to his queen.

This stone of the inner life can sometimes cause us to brood and feel moody. It can also cause a spiritual intoxication that the amethyst can heal. The name black agate is sometimes mistakenly given to jet, and obsidian is often called Icelandic agate.

Crimson agate: The color of nobility and wealth for the Romans, crimson symbolizes the elevation of the spirit, as well as sadness, blood, and death. It is the stone of cameo engravers and artists. It also represents their destiny, for better or for worse. This stone is one of energetic action, will, and relentlessness.

Green agate: This stone symbolizes hope for the future and growth, evolution, germination, and fertility. It is the stone of the creative imagination. It also represents fatality and temptation. The Tartarus idol, a statue of green agate with seven featherless arrows in his silver hand, tormented St. Anthony during his painful visions.

Colorless agate: This stone represents earthly solidity and love of the nurturing soil.

Therapeutic Uses

Agates represent life in its most earthly, material aspect. This stone should be worn against the skin. Recommended for pregnant women, it enhances pregnancy and birth. It helps women avoid the "baby blues" new mothers often experience after giving birth. An agate jewel worn between the breasts activates lactation. It also has a noticeable effect on male sexual problems. For neurasthenics and people suffering from depression, this "life stone" has proven to be very effective. Look at a translucent agate after you have worn it against your skin, and see the light play with its different colors and veins.

Agates cure fevers: a cold stone placed on one's forehead is generally effective. However, if the fever returns, consult a doctor. Agate also reduces the symptoms of epilepsy. For some people, it guards against sleepwalking. The German mystic Hildegard of Bingen recommended it for heart ailments, and also for everything concerning the heart and emotions. She recommended wearing a disk in the middle of the chest to strengthen the cardiac muscle. Agate also helps to treat wounds by slowing down the flow of blood, and it relieves itching due to insect stings and bites. Moss agate, named for its mosslike appearance, cures buzzing in the ears and intestinal cramps.

The agate's effects can be very powerful. Those suffering from depression or in mourning should avoid this stone. In addition, agates with an empty center (geodes and hollow stones) may accentuate the feeling of helplessness and despair.

In general, agates protect people against traffic accidents and other problems when traveling. Agates with regular designs will help those who desire peace and harmony. However, stones having irregular designs may have the reverse effect; these stones can stimulate us to take effective action and help us to make important decisions.

Zodiac Correspondences

This earthy stone will give Taurus a satisfying feeling of stability. It will help Scorpio to open up spiritually. Yellow agate will help Virgos attract members of the opposite sex. Native Americans believe moss agate is linked to the sign of Gemini.

ALABASTER

Chemical composition: Calcium sulfate

Color: White, pink, sometimes brownish

Principal deposits: Alabaster is found just about everywhere, but the legendary alabaster of the ancient statues and objects came from a deposit near Volterra in Tuscany (Italy).

Hardness: 2

Density: 2.3

Etymology and General Characteristics

From the Latin *albus,* or "white," Alabaster is not the "poor person's marble" as it is often claimed.

The smooth texture and white color of this stone evoke the sensual beauty of the human body. This stone represents the "prison" of the body as opposed to the freedom of the spirit. Alabaster represents the inner life that often smolders under coldness or apparent inertia.

The myth of Galatea, sculpted in alabaster by Pygmalion who wanted his statue to come to life, is good symbolism for this stone. It was the canon for female shapes, as much for its appearance as for its whiteness. The poetic cliché "breasts of alabaster" is still used today. It shows how connected this stone is with the flesh.

Roman women made a powder out of it to whiten their cleavage. This powder was also an ingredient in foundation makeup in the ancient world.

Therapeutic Uses

Alabaster powder has a softening effect on the skin similar to talcum powder. The calcium contained in alabaster would be as effective as talcum, but because it's often impure and can contain other, more toxic substances, it's better not to use it.

Alabaster powder diluted in distilled water relieves mental disorders. Mood swings can be reduced by drinking a glass of water with a teaspoon of powder in it every morning for a week. Alabaster, a female stone, also helps with menstrual disorders.

Because of its ability to regenerate the skin, alabaster is good for tightening loose muscles. An alabaster stone can be used to gently massage double chins and drooping eyelids.

Zodiac Correspondences

The dilemma for those born under the sign of Aquarius is the pull between freedom and service—the desire to serve others, and the desire to be free at all costs. Alabaster can help to balance these two contradictory impulses.

Pisces will feel more confident when wearing this stone. Alabaster will bring emotional warmth to Virgo and Libra.

AMAZONITE

Chemical composition: Aluminum and potassium double silicate

Color: Green and blue-green

Principal deposits: The Amazon (where it gets its name), India, and Madagascar

Hardness: 6 to 6.5

Density: 2.5

Etymology and General Characteristics

The stone's name comes from the principal region where it is found. The conquistadors found amazonite and had it cut into jewels and cult objects. This stone is connected to the legend of the Amazon women and served as a medication for those formidable female soldiers for lesions and illnesses of all kinds.

This stone's energy remains tempered by its color. While primarily a war stone, the blue-green color regulates the aggressive aspects and stimulates us to seek emotional balance.

Therapeutic Uses

Legend has it that some Amazon women had one breast removed so they could more effectively practice archery. Afterward, they rubbed their wounds with a polished amazonite to avoid infection. Amazonite soothes rashes and heals blisters, like those of chicken pox or smallpox. It also heals acne and relieves the pain of rheumatism and osteoarthritis. It is important to note that this stone does not heal illnesses that require in-depth treatment; it only relieves the painful effects.

Amazonite is also used to treat sexual disorders—lack of desire, impotence, vaginitis, sexual obsession, and priapism (a prolonged and painful erection).

Zodiac Correspondences

The royal signs of Leo and Aries have an affinity with this stone. It can be used to treat depression in Scorpios.

AMBER

Chemical composition: Amber is not a stone, but a fossilized, resinous substance that has a vegetal origin.

Color: Gold or green

Principal deposits: The Baltic area, the North Sea, Romania, Italy (Sicily), Myanmar (Burma), and the Dominican Republic

Hardness: 2 to 2.5

Density: 1 to 1.1

Etymology and General Characteristics

The word *amber* comes from the Arab *anbar,* which is derived from the word *ambergris* (a secretion from the sperm whale with a musk odor, used in perfume). The Greek word for amber is *elektron,* the origin of the words *electron* and *electricity* in French and English. Amber's magnetic properties were discovered and described by the Greek philosopher Thales around 600 BCE.

In the form of a jewel or rosary, amber acts as an energy charger. It discharges the overabundant energy or bad moods of the person wearing it. While some people claim that dark-colored amber is more effective than light amber, this has never been verified. Jet is often mistakenly referred to as "black amber." Amber is often imitated. To verify its authenticity, test its electrical properties by tearing up little pieces of paper and rubbing the amber on a wool cloth. If it is genuine, the paper should be drawn to it in the same way that iron is drawn by a magnet.

Amber is a symbol of longevity and many have centuries-old insects or shells enclosed in their resin. The French novelist and playwright Honoré Balzac wrote of "amber in the heart of which an insect lives eternally in its immutable beauty." It is also the symbol of loneliness and nostalgia. Apollo, banished from Olympus, shed "tears of amber." Medieval goldsmiths combined amber with garnets to make beautiful jewelry. This combination brings balance and meditative wisdom to its fieriness and vitality. It is the harmonious alliance of the physical and the mental, the corporal and the spiritual.

Purity and holiness are evoked by amber. The faces of saints and wise men were once described as "the color of amber." The Celtic warrior Ogmios was said to have led his followers around with chains of gold and amber. Amber also represents the spiritual connection that frees people, as opposed to the material chains that imprison them.

Therapeutic Uses

A veritable electric battery, amber helps us recharge our energies. It's possible to practice a kind of electrotherapy by rubbing amber on a wool cloth and bringing it close to a sick or painful part of your body. You will hear cracks and may even see sparks. You can also place amber on your body, wait for the resin to warm to body temperature, and leave it there for about 20 minutes.

Amber both strengthens us and makes us energetic. It effectively fights against depression and anxiety. Amber is also renowned for helping to cure impotence and frigidity. Once ground into powder and taken in the form of pills, it is said to "electrify" desire. You can make your own powder by rubbing the amber against a nutmeg grater. To use, mix the powder with food.

Amber is the protective stone for children. A piece of amber sewn into the clothes of an unweaned infant will reduce his teething pains. Rub the baby's gums with saffron water—this spice is amber's phyto-therapeutic complement. According to medieval beliefs, amber smoke chases away bad spirits. It could be used to purify the ambient air if it weren't so expensive!

Zodiac Correspondences

The qualities of amber are in harmony with Gemini. Its power and purity also make it a good fit for Leo and Virgo.

AMETHYST

Chemical composition: Silicon dioxide

Color: The color of this quartz ranges from wine-colored lilac to deep blue purple, according to its concentration of manganese and iron. Green or reddish brown amethysts are more rare.

Principal deposits: Brazil, Uruguay, Sri Lanka, Maghreb (North Africa), and Russia (Ural Mountains)

Hardness: 7

Density: 2.65

Etymology and General Characteristics

The Greek word *ametusthos* means "not intoxicated." This stone is connected to temperance. This sobriety was originally of a spiritual nature. "The ferrymen of souls," the church administrators, needed to be clear-headed to manage their dioceses. Kissing the priests' amethyst ring kept them from mystical intoxication.

The ancient philosopher Pliny the Elder found that an amethyst bearing figures engraved with the moon and the sun immunized people against poisons. Amethyst is connected to the Temperance card in the tarot, representing balance.

According to Ovid, Amethyst was a nymph pursued by Bacchus. Wanting to escape from him, she called on Diana. The goddess came to her rescue by transforming her into a shiny stone, in "pure, cold crystal." Bacchus, furious, threw his glass filled with wine on this stone, which gave it its colorful hue.

Amethyst benefits from the properties of the manganese it contains. A stone conducive to mediation, it enhances creativity, strengthens our imagination and intuition, and refines our thinking—all of which allows us to bring new projects to fruition. Used as a talisman, the amethyst helps us to focus, making success possible.

Amethyst is the "couple's stone," the stone of our intimate dualities and our relationship to our partners. A symbol of spiritual purity, it can give meaning to a union based at first on the flesh that withers away little by little, for lack of other kinds of communion. It makes it possible to transcend the carnal union and connect more deeply.

Therapeutic Uses

Amethyst is used to treat psychic disturbances, stress, and nervous tension. When placed on the forehead, it soothes migraine headaches and diminishes neurotic conditions. An amethyst, placed under your pillow or mattress, will cure insomnia and stimulate pleasant dreams. Amethyst powder can be used to make ointments that activate blood circulation.

An amethyst placed on the navel can protect a person from intoxication and help cure alcoholism (in conjunction with other treatments such as counseling). Navel piercings make it possible to always keep an amethyst on this spot. Amethyst is also used to cure sexual problems. Finally, an amethyst can help to soothe burns and calm angry temperaments. It is also the stone of diplomats, negotiators, and businesspeople.

Zodiac Correspondences

People born in Pisces, a water sign, and a symbol of Christ, are in harmony with amethyst. It relates to the purity of Virgo and the strength of Aries. It enhances intuition in Sagittarius and Capricorn.

AMETRINE

Chemical composition: Silicon dioxide

Color: Purple and yellow

Principal deposits: Ametrine is a rare stone found in amethyst deposits

Hardness: 7

Density: 2.6

Etymology and General Characteristics

The name *ametrine* is a combination of the words *amethyst* and *citrine*. This stone relates to the Sahasrara or seventh chakra on the top of our heads. It connects us to the cosmos and enhances the perception of hidden phenomena, psychic waves, and currents. It is conducive to the dynamism of active meditation.

Therapeutic Uses

Ametrine is useful for all digestive problems—most notably, gas, colic, and liver ailments. Ametrine is an invigorating stone that enhances good moods and reduces the effects of anger and defeatism.

Zodiac Correspondences

Ametrine will produce drive in Pisces and calm the often abrupt nature of Aries. It will have a balancing effect on Sagittarius and Virgo.

ANDALUSITE

Chemical composition: Aluminum silicate

Color: Green, yellow-green, gray, or reddish brown

Principal deposits: Brazil, Sri Lanka, Russia (Ural Mountains), North America, and Spain (Andalusia)

Hardness: 7.5

Density: 3.1

Etymology and General Characteristics

A clear variety of andalusite was first found in Andalusia, Spain. Amazonite's European sister, andalusite, resembles it from a symbolic point of view. However, it represents a more piquant, tense energy. Andalusite is a stone of fieriness, vigor, and generosity.

Therapeutic Uses

The same as amazonite (and of many stones composed of aluminum) but with a less durable effect.

Andalusite will "attack" the problem and the potassium of amazonite will then "weigh down" the force of the aluminum. Be careful, however, for this two-stone treatment sometimes produces a slight intoxication or vertigo over a period of several hours.

Zodiac Correspondences

Amazonite strengthens the determination and perseverance of Scorpio. This stone will provide emotional balance for sensitive Pisces.

AQUAMARINE

Chemical composition: Aluminum and beryllium silicon; a variety of emerald containing traces of lithium, fluoride, and calcium that changes its color

Color: Blue or blue-green

Principal deposits: The American continent, South Africa, Nigeria, Madagascar, and Russia (Ural Mountains)

Hardness: 7.5 to 8

Density: 2.7

Etymology and General Characteristics

The stone's name comes from *aqua,* the Latin word for "water," and *marine,* and this watery blue stone evokes the sea. It's also described as "murky" blue-green, a word that once had a positive meaning. People often confuse Oriental aquamarine, a variety of topaz, with aquamarine.

Aquamarine embodies all the symbols connected to the sea, and also, in a lesser way, that which relates to heaven reflected on the surface of the water. It presents itself as a sort of mirror, reflecting itself indefinitely. This stone makes it possible to discover the hidden meaning of reality. It is conducive for meditation and the awakening of our paranormal abilities. It is a stone of correspondences and symmetries—the stone of prophets, shamans, healers, and mystics. For some, aquamarine induces revelations. Some traditions claim that you can see your guardian angel through an aquamarine stone when it points to the north.

This stone also enables us to explore the darkest depths of our souls. This is the ideal stone for psychologists, psychiatrists, and psychoanalysts to wear on their index fingers. This clarity puts us face to face with ourselves—and others. It is often dangerous. If the purification is too harsh, it can bring on lucid vertigo.

Aquamarine is also a stone of love and fidelity.

Therapeutic Uses

This is the stone of the breath, the respiratory tracts, and the lungs. It can heal sinus conditions and frequent coughing. It is also effective for hay fever and other chronic allergies. Asthma, the aftereffects of whooping cough, and diphtheria can be relieved by combining aquamarine with an emerald and a green jade, or with a tourmaline.

Sucking on an uncut or polished piece of aquamarine can relieve a toothache. Tired eyes and some vision problems will be reduced or relieved by lying down and applying aquamarine to the eyelids for 20 minutes every night before going to bed. Putting a stone on your stomach or the liver area will help with problems in these organs. Placed on the solar plexus, aquamarine's beneficial action will calm down nervous spasms. Some skin diseases caused by allergies are also cured by aquamarine. It can complement the treatment for shingles through its organic and psychological action.

Zodiac Correspondences

A water stone, aquamarine is connected to Pisces and Aquarius, the sign of the water bearer. It is also connected to the signs of Gemini and Libra.

ARAGONITE

Chemical composition: Calcium, strontium, or barium

Color: White

Principal deposits: This stone is common on all continents.

Hardness: 3.5 to 4

Density: 2.9

Etymology and General Characteristics

Aragonite gets its name from the province of Aragon in Spain. Various kinds of aragonite knickknacks were once made there.

Mother-of-pearl is composed of aragonite. Aragonite is also the main element in the shell of many mollusks and corals. Pearls are made out of it, as are "cavern pearls," aragonite concretions that are found in caves. Aragonite is less common than calcite.

Therapeutic Uses

Aragonite gets activated when in contact with the skin and can strengthen the effect of medicinal calcium. This stone is a catalyst that strengthens the effects of the other gemstones rather than a specific remedy for a particular type of infection. In addition, it stabilizes and intensifies our inner radiance.

Zodiac Correspondences

Water signs will feel in harmony with aragonite, and this harmony will spill over to the people around them. Cancers and Pisces, in particular, will find it easier to share their inner richness. Aragonite will give Virgos the daring energy they often lack. It will lessen the effect of Capricorn's fierce individualism.

AVENTURINE

Chemical composition: Silicum dioxide, a variety of quartz or feld-spar containing inclusions of mica, oligistis iron, and fuchsite

Color: Glittering green, blue, gray, or a golden reddish brown; this stone can be opaque or translucent.

Principal deposits: Russia (Ural Mountains, Siberia), Brazil, India, and Madagascar

Hardness: 7

Density: 2.6

Etymology and General Characteristics

Until the nineteenth century, aventurine was called the "stone of the Amazons." In fact, the Brazilian deposits were said to have supplied jewels and talismans for those formidable female warriors. It was also known as "sunstone" or "silver rain." In Italian, it was known as "*all'avventura.*" Legend has it that in 1700, a worker in an Italian glassmaking shop accidentally dropped brass filings into a melting glass vat. The result, once it cooled down, was appealing and people used it to make jewelry. The name *aventurine* was later applied to the natural stone, which looks like the industrial product.

Aventurine leads us toward inner harmony. It soothes the mind and enhances self-healing. It helps us to better understand nature and to commune with the forests and the oceans. It makes it possible to deeply absorb the soothing vibrations of the countryside. At the same time, aventurine, especially the green stone, calms the agitation caused by hectic schedules and the stress of big city living. A stone for achieving equilibrium, it helps to correct the tendency toward defeatism, submissiveness, and passivity—especially the brown aventurine.

Therapeutic Uses

Green aventurine activates the physical growth of children and teenagers. It can even correct certain growth retardation. It enhances the intellectual development of young people who are struggling with schoolwork and destructive hyperactivity. In addition, it greatly diminishes the effects of acne, a source of worry for teenagers. However, it can't counteract the effects of an unbalanced diet.

Blue aventurine, which is rarer than the green stone, has the same effects but it seems to act faster. Aventurine works wonders on quick-tempered or brutal temperaments. It can greatly diminish the effects of domestic strife between spouses.

Aventurine water (made by soaking a stone fragment in demineralized water overnight) is beneficial for fighting eczema, rosacea, juvenile acne, and other skin problems. This water can be drunk or used in ablutions.

Aventurine is mainly the "heart stone." You must wear it on your chest to feel its positive effects. By soothing the mind, the stone helps to generate the energy needed to heal a weak or defective myocardium. It will restore rhythm and strength in the motor muscles. It has a very good effect on hair and the suprarenal glands. This stone also fights stress and improves memory. It is sometimes spelled *avanturine*.

Zodiac Correspondences

Aventurine's ability to calm the mind makes it particularly beneficial for the moody water signs—Pisces, Scorpio, and especially Cancer. Its serene quality has a balancing effect on fiery Sagittarius. The brute strength and organic power of red aventurine has an affinity with Taurus.

AZURITE

Chemical composition: Basic copper carbonate

Color: Bright blue

Principal deposits: France, Russia (Ural Mountains), Brazil, United States (Arizona, Pennsylvania), and Mexico

Hardness: 3.5

Density: 3.7 to 3.9

Etymology and General Characteristics

This stone gets its name from its deep blue color. A soft stone, it is easily reduced to powder. When mixed with linseed oil, it produces a whole range of beautiful shades of blue used by painters.

Therapeutic Uses

Azurite was once mixed with alcohol and dabbed on the throats of people suffering from angina. It is not to be confused with blue methylene that served the same purpose. Azurite's effects are long lasting. This blue stone refines, sharpens, and soothes. It strengthens the therapeutic qualities of all other blue stones.

For general well-being or to enhance the effects of other blue stones, crush a pea-size fragment of azurite and pour it into a liter of distilled water (never mineral or spring water!). Let it rest for a night. Take a teaspoon of this water every morning and every evening for a week. The rest should not be consumed but applied with a cotton tip on a painful or injured area. The effects of the copper will be expressed for the greatest good of the patient's health.

Zodiac Correspondences

Azurite will soothe the sore throats of those born in the sign of Sagittarius. It will also stimulate their natural interest in philosophy.

Taurus's sore throats will also be healed by this stone. It will give people born under this sign additional self-control and self-confidence.

BERYL

Chemical composition: Aluminum and beryllium silicate

Color: Pale yellow or yellowish green, according to its concentration of iron

Principal deposits: Beryl is a common stone found just about everywhere in the world.

Hardness: 7.5 to 8

Density: 2.6 to 2.8

Etymology and General Characteristics

From the Greek word *beryllos,* which is derived from a language of ancient India. This word has given us the German word *brille,* meaning "glasses," and the French word *bésicles,* or "spectacles." Transparent beryl, like the pale emerald, was once used to make the polished lenses for magnifying glasses.

A mineral used to make cement, it is also used as a stone in construction. As a powder, it is spread on fields to enrich the soil. According to its color, various varieties of beryl can be distinguished:

Bixbite: Unknown origin. Pale pink to salmon colored. Sometimes red bordering on light brown.

Goshenite: From Goshen, a city in Massachusetts where a colorless deposit is found.

Heliodore: This golden yellow stone is called "gift of the sun" from the Greek word *helios,* meaning "sun." It is found in Madagascar and Brazil. Some heliodores get their sustained yellow color from the presence of uranium. They are slightly radioactive but not dangerous at such a low dose.

Morganite: The name comes from J. P. Morgan, an American billionaire and gemstone collector. "Peachtree flower" or pink mauve in color.

Therapeutic Uses

Beryl is generally beneficial for one's health. This inexpensive stone is sometimes called the "panacea for poor people." Beryl invigorates one's visual acuteness and makes it not only possible to see better but also to observe, to notice what seems significant—and insignificant. It is the stone of "antique hunters," dealers of secondhand goods and antiques who know how to discover rare objects in a batch of dusty horrors. It is the stone of prospectors, of gold—or precious stone—hunters who will find the rare gemstone in the most disorganized, muddy jumble. It is also the talisman of the doctor confronted with a difficult case and a complicated diagnosis.

Zodiac Correspondences

Beryl will calm the tendency of those born under the sign of Taurus to blindly charge ahead. The stone will help Cancers to see themselves clearly without the emotional fog that often surrounds this sign.

CALCITE

Chemical composition: Calcium carbonate

Color: This stone has sides shaped like a diamond, or irregular triangles. It may be blue, green, red, gray, colorless, brown, or black.

Principal deposits: Calcite is relatively common. It is found in Western Europe, France (Provence and the Vosges Mountains), Romania, Madagascar, United States, and Egypt.

Hardness: 3

Density: 2.5 to 3

Etymology and General Characteristics

Calcite gets its name from lime and calcium. It has their energetic qualities and can also serve as a purifier. This stone is conducive to calmness and tolerance. It has a "yin" or feminine quality that also relates to men.

Therapeutic Uses

The calcium in calcite gets activated when it comes in contact with the skin, and it strengthens the effects of medicinal calcium. Calcite fights all kinds of pain. Roll a calcite pearl all along the affected bones.

You can also dissolve calcite in vinegar. Anxiety and depression can be treated by rubbing your temples lightly with the vinegar solution. Calcite can also be used as a sexual stimulant.

Zodiac Correspondences

Calcite is a stone of revelation. It helps us find our inner richness. It is especially harmonious with the water signs Cancer and Pisces. It can help them discover their hidden potential and their secret or unsatisfied desires. Capricorn will find a bit of much needed serenity and Virgo, Leo, Libra, and Sagittarius will appreciate both its stimulating and calming effects.

CARNELIAN

Chemical composition: Silicon dioxide

Color: This single color quartz is a variety of agate without stains. It is light or dark orange in color.

Principal deposits: Uruguay, Japan, Brazil, Russia (Siberia), India, and North Africa

Hardness: 6.5 to 7

Density: 2.6

Etymology and General Characteristics

From the Latin *corneus,* or horn, with two suffixes: *-alis* and *-ina.* This has given us the word *cornouiller,* or "dogwood." In fact, carnelian does resemble that shrub's fruit. It is the stone of dawn and twilight. It is very positive and can inspire us during the early stages of an important project. It can also aid the person who is looking back at the end of a full life, and appreciating the lessons learned. It "brings the past up-to-date" and simultaneously prepares us for the future. It enhances our ability to "look inside" and makes us lucid and benevolent. Carnelian's therapeutic aspects are similar to those of agate but carnelian differs from it by its warmer aura. It is the stone of enterprise, and of appreciating the fullness of a life well lived.

Therapeutic Uses

Carnelian clarifies the voice: it is the singer's stone. It also purifies the blood and is beneficial for all illnesses having to do with circulation—congestion, phlebitis, varicose veins, and hemorrhoids. It also cures boils and skin irritations. Placed on the solar plexus or at the navel level, carnelian will help with digestion. Bilious or liver problems will also be relieved. Sexual problems will be healed by applying a carnelian stone to the genital organs. You can also gently rub areas affected with rheumatism. Carnelian accelerates scarification and heals nosebleeds. If these recur, however, you should consult a doctor.

Zodiac Correspondences

Red carnelian can help those born under the sign of Aries to launch new projects. But be aware: it can also enhance their quick-tempered tendencies. This stone should be used with caution. The red carnelian will have an energetic, reassuring effect on Virgo and Cancer. Geminis will find the yellow carnelian both invigorating and balancing.

CELESTINE

Chemical composition: Strontium sulfate

Color: This stone is most often blue or colorless, but it can also be found with a green, brown, or red cast.

Principal deposits: Canada, Madagascar, and Italy (Sicily). This stone is often found with aragonite.

Hardness: 3 to 3.5

Density: 3.9 to 4

Etymology and General Characteristics

This stone gets its name from the blue sky. In Sicily, celestine is the result of a slow transformation of sulfur gypsum. It is used in rockets, fireworks, and even certain munitions. Celestine's combustion produces an intense red light. Its composition also enables it to be used in manufacturing sugar for molasses and handmade candy. Last of all, its intense color is used as a coloring agent for paints, ceramics, and in glassmaking.

Therapeutic Uses

Like many blue stones, celestine stimulates spiritual maturity. This color represents tranquility and balance.

This stone will bring fevers down and it can aid in the treatment of malaria. It makes an excellent stimulant for a long-term course of treatment but it cannot heal complex illnesses by itself.

It also fights against skin infections and rashes. Placing it on the Anja or sixth chakra can bring about a noticeable improvement in vision.

Zodiac Correspondences

Celestine reduces depression in Cancer and stimulates spiritual maturity in Gemini. It invigorates Aquarius and relieves Sagittarius's chronic digestive problems. The stone should be placed directly on the stomach.

CHALCEDONY

Chemical composition: Silicon dioxide

Color: This stone can be gray, milky white, pink, blue, or light blue.

Principal deposits: South and West Africa, Brazil, Uruguay, Madagascar, India, Russia (Siberia), and United States

Hardness: 7

Density: 2.6

Etymology and General Characteristics

This stone's name comes from that of the city of Chalcedony in Bythinia, known for its deposits of copper (*calchos* in Greek), which was located across from Byzantium, in modern day Istanbul.

Far from shouts and furor, chalcedony encourages reflection and meditation. Its gentle radiance prepares us for action but also helps us to hold back words we might regret. It is the speaker's stone, the stone of one who must measure his words. It is said that the great Roman orator Cicero used to wear one around his neck. The quartz and the silica give both a fibrous and a granular microcrystalline structure to this stone.

Therapeutic Uses

Just touching this stone with the tip of your tongue will enable you to be a good political speaker. Lawyers should suck on it, like candy, while listening to their opponent's arguments. They will then be in good shape to counter them. Actors should rub it against their lips and throat. Singers can drink a glass of water in which a chalcedony stone has soaked for an hour before going out on stage.

Wearing a chalcedony stone around your neck will enable you to overcome stage fright and the fear of public speaking. Thanks to chalcedony, you'll be saved from the disappointing experience of coming up with an answer too late.

This stone is used to treat chronic hoarseness and inflammation of the throat. It protects us against weakness, bad moods, obsessive jealousy, and depression. It reduces sleepwalking. It soothes chilblains and protects against problems while traveling.

Zodiac Correspondences

Chalcedony will help Taurus to accept and appreciate the ideas of others.

White chalcedony's calming influence is very favorable for Cancer. But be aware that too much calm can sometimes be harmful.

Gemini will be better off with the blue varieties. But be careful: a tendency to stay "in the clouds" can be activated by chalcedony. It is best to add a complementary red stone.

Chalcedony water or a white chalcedony stone mounted as a ring will have a balancing effect on Sagittarius. Choose silver rather than gold, nickel silver, or brass for the ring's setting.

CHRYSOBERYL

Chemical composition: Beryllium aluminate

Color: Yellow, gold, or greenish yellow

Principal deposits: Madagascar, Brazil, Sri Lanka, Myanmar (Burma), Russia (Ural Mountains), and Zimbabwe

Hardness: 8.5

Density: 3.7

Etymology and General Characteristics

From *khrusos,* which means "gold" in Greek, and from *beryllos,* meaning "beryl." This beautiful stone is said to strengthen romantic feelings. It will help us to remain faithful if given by our partner in the form of an amulet. It also strengthens intuition.

Alexandrite, a double stone, is a variety of chrysoberyl. It owes its name to Czar Alexander II who admired it. This stone, which is yellow-green in the light of day, becomes crimson by candlelight or electric light.

Therapeutic Uses

Chrysoberyl balances arterial tension. Because of this, it can cure eye problems due to corneal arterioles.

The therapeutic qualities of alexandrite vary—alternating between traits similar to those of jade and emerald and those of garnet and ruby.

It is best to leave this rare stone to an experienced lithotherapist.

Zodiac Correspondences

Chrysoberyl will help Taurus, that ardent go-getter, to be more sensitive to the feelings and needs of others. Meditating on a chrysoberyl stone will help Cancers to keep their feet on the ground and enhance their concentration.

CHRYSOCOLLA

Chemical composition: Copper hydrosilicate or malachite silicate

Color: Blue-green

Principal deposits: This stone is found in copper deposits. Chile, Russia (Ural mountains), southwestern Africa, United States, and Italy are the main producers.

Hardness: 2 to 4 (according to the proportion of copper and other metals)

Density: 2.2

Etymology and General Characteristics

Again, from the Greek *khrusos,* meaning "gold" (because of the shininess of the copper in this stone). Chrysocolla was used in antiquity in the practice of metallurgy, and as a supplement in melting down metals.

It is the stone of forgiveness, peace, and the strengthening of emotional bonds. It encourages compassion. It helps us recover our natural spontaneity.

One strange property of chrysocolla has been known since antiquity: it encourages people to stay at home. People with wandering temperaments, those who never stay in one place, will benefit from it. It is the stone of monks, hermits—and prisoners. It diminishes the anxiety and depression that often accompanies seclusion.

Therapeutic Uses

Chrysocolla is often confused with turquoise and its therapeutic uses are similar. This stone's calming influence helps with nervous disorders such as anxiety, depression, feelings of guilt, and hyperkinetic movement.

Chrysocolla is a beneficial stone for women. It reduces menstrual pain and is conducive to happy pregnancies by relieving the anxieties of first-time mothers. Placing the stone on the belly at the ovaries or uterus is very effective. Its calming action is also conducive to a harmonious birth. Holding a chrysocolla stone will reduce the pain of labor.

Zodiac Correspondences

Chrysocolla is often linked with Taurus. However, its affinity with peace-loving Libra is even more pronounced. It will help Sagittarius to forgive, and calm anxiety in those born under the sign of Aquarius.

CHRYSOLITE

Chemical composition: Ferrous magnesium silicate

Color: Sparkling, brilliant colors—yellow-green, olive, or brown

Principal deposits: The Red Sea, Australia, Patagonia, and United States (Nevada)

Hardness: 6.5 to 7

Density: 3.2 to 3.3

Etymology and General Characteristics

From the Greek *khrusos* (gold) and *lithos* (stone). It is the "golden stone" but not just because of the color of some varieties. It's the stone of joy, the sun, and nature in all its bounty.

Therapeutic Uses

Chrysolite stimulates the nervous system, regulates the cardiac rhythm, and normalizes arterial tension.

A powerful purifier, it helps to discharge gallstones and stimulates the kidneys. To be used with the changing of the seasons.

Zodiac Correspondences

The fire signs of Leo and Aries will benefit from the power of this "petrified sun." Stroking this stone before acting helps Aries natives channel their energy into positive, beautiful actions. Scorpio will rediscover the joy of living by holding this stone.

CHRYSOPRASE

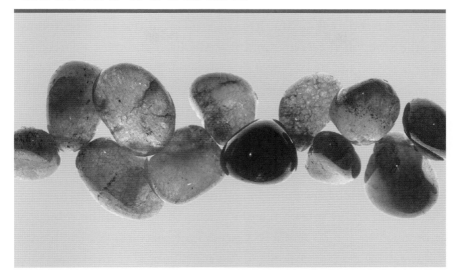

Chemical composition: Silicon dioxide

Color: Due to the presence of nickel, this stone can be light green or olive-colored. Chrysoprase is usually opaque but some stones are translucent.

Principal deposits: South Africa, Russia (Ural Mountains), Chile, and Poland (Silesia, next to the city of Frankenstein!)

Hardness: 7

Density: 2.6

Etymology and General Characteristics

This stone is actually a variety of chalcedony. Its name comes from the Greek *khrusos* (gold) and *prasos* (leek), reflecting its color and its relationship with the leek's digestive and other beneficial qualities. Leeks were often used in the ancient pharmacopoeia. Leeks are good for the vocal cords, and Cicero, the great Roman orator whose nickname was "porophage" (leek eater), ate a lot of this vegetable and carried a chalcedony—perhaps a chrysoprase—with him at all times.

It was also a symbol of victory: the Egyptian pharaoh Cheops rewarded his most valiant warriors by offering them handfuls of leeks, which corresponded to the Roman crowns of laurels. Chrysoprase was the stone of the Franks and it symbolized the spirit of freedom, adventure, and the conquests of this Germanic tribe.

Chalcedony is also connected to femininity. Its calm strength and gentleness are its two most distinctive qualities. The qualities of chalcedony are even stronger in chrysoprase.

Therapeutic Uses

Refer to those of chalcedony. In addition, chrysoprase can have a beneficial effect on the urinary tract by placing the stone on the kidneys or at the bladder for 20 minutes. Chrysoprase increases self-confidence. It normalizes arterial tension and can contribute to curing some vision problems. It also helps us to develop our gifts and forces us to do the work necessary to succeed.

Zodiac Correspondences

Chrysoprase is very favorable to Cancer. This stone, worn as a jewel, will help Gemini natives express themselves clearly. It will reduce the need for victory in the proud lion Leo.

CITRINE

Chemical composition: Silicon dioxide, in the quartz family

Color: The colors of this beautiful, semiprecious stone range from lemon to brownish yellow. Its structure gives it the appearance of a yellow-colored amethyst.

Principal deposits: Brazil, Madagascar, England, and Spain (Iberian Peninsula)

Hardness: 7

Density: 2.6

Etymology and General Characteristics

Citrine gets its name from its lemon yellow color. Like this citrus fruit, it is invigorating and energizing. Citrine's radiance adds a certain gentleness to its reinvigorating strength. Although it can help us to find fullness and inner peace, it also has the capacity to encourage us to action.

It strengthens our inner light and stimulates us to manifest our dreams. This stone strengthens creativity and is ideal for artists of all kinds. It is also the stone of the warrior, the conqueror. Like a miniature sun, this stone is infused with energy that can be used for beneficial— or destructive—ends.

It can exacerbate aggressiveness in some. This noble, powerful stone should be handled with care! It should not be worn with other stones.

Because of its color, citrine is sometimes called safranite, or fake topaz. By heating up amethysts, forgers are able to change the color and pass the stones off as the more costly citrine. Citrine shares many of its qualities with amber.

Therapeutic Uses

By activating nervous impulses, citrine can act in the best or worst ways. It strengthens intelligence and the intellectual faculties of concentration and wisdom. It can be used to prepare for a test. It also activates the functions of the endocrine glands.

Citrine stimulates digestion but is not recommended for the treatment of ulcers. By harmonizing digestion, it helps keep the skin, nails, and hair healthy. It also helps to regulate the secretion of insulin, but it cannot be used to treat diabetes. It can be used, however, to energize the standard treatments. Citrine water (obtained by soaking a stone in a glass of water for 20 minutes) will help chronically ill people have more energy. Combining citrine and amber relieves asthma and reduces many allergies.

Citrine is not recommended for those with an aggressive, fiery, quick-tempered nature. Similarly, people with a tendency to slander or gossip should avoid this stone.

Zodiac Correspondences

Citrine's beneficial aspects are suitable for all the signs. In the same way, its dangerous aspects can harm them all.

For Taurus, this stone can help alleviate feelings of anxiety and fear. (During periods when these feelings are heightened, Taurus will benefit from wearing a citrine ring or pendant for a few days.)

Citrine will stimulate Leo's creative faculties, and give Virgos and Libras a boost of confidence and optimism. This stone will help those born under the sign of Gemini to better understand their sometimes contradictory feelings and needs.

CORAL

Chemical composition: Limestone

Color: In its natural state, coral can appear dull. Polishing it reveals a shiny, red-orange beauty.

Principal deposits: Coral beds may occupy large surfaces. The biggest concentration can be found in the warm seas near Torre del Greco, in Naples, Italy.

Hardness: 3 to 4

Density: 2.6 to 2.7

Etymology and General Characteristics

Coral protects us from negative influences. It regulates our feelings and purifies our thoughts. Coral has a pivotal place in the marine world. It cannot survive in polluted waters; as a result, it reflects the general health of the sea.

Connected to blood by its red color, coral is also connected to the viscera through its twisted shapes. The Greeks saw the blood of the

Medusa in the coral and believed that one couldn't gaze at it without being changed into stone. Perseus decapitated Medusa, and from this blood Pegasus, the winged horse, was born.

Coral symbolically includes the three kingdoms: animal, vegetable, and mineral. It was believed to turn away thunder and stop hemorrhages. For the ancient Irish, it was connected to women's mouths—and words—by its red color.

Goldsmiths of the baroque era mixed coral with gold, silver, and other stones to create a variety of grotesque effigies, chimera, and demons.

Therapeutic Uses

Coral concerns everything that relates to blood circulation, such as anemia and other circulation problems. Coral fights anorexia and heals disorders that stem from malnutrition. Menstrual pains, and other symptoms of PMS, are reduced by using coral. In general, wearing coral jewelry can bring energy, hope, and vitality. Coral can be used as a seasoning for meals by grinding it and mixing the powder with vinegar. The mixture will foam up during preparation.

Zodiac Correspondences

Taurus should use brown coral rather than red. It will enable those born under this sign to better control their emotions.

The red-colored coral will energize and make Cancer feel more adventurous. Wearing a pink coral ring will give Libras the confidence to speak their minds. This marine mineral is the perfect stone for Pisces; it can provide a sense of stability for this watery sign. Coral will also have a grounding effect on Aries.

CRYSTAL:
CATHEDRAL CRYSTAL

Chemical composition: Silicon dioxide

Color: Transparent or milky white

Principal deposits: France (Alps), Madagascar, United States (Arkansas), Russia (Ural Mountains), and Brazil

Hardness: 7

Density: 2.65

Etymology and General Characteristics

The name "cathedral" comes from the fact that this crystal's tips evoke the spires of Gothic architecture. It is also called "crystal comb" because its tips can be oriented in all directions. Cathedral crystals are found in flint slate. They are sought after because of their rarity and beauty. The play of light, refracted in all directions, makes it a true spectacle to behold—its iridescence and sparkle can be seen as the stone is moved.

This stone is particularly conducive for meditation, reflection, and prayer. When using this stone for meditation, it is recommended that you point the largest tip toward the constellation that corresponds to your zodiac sign. You can also choose your rising sign. In that case, it is better to get the advice of an experienced lithotherapist beforehand.

Therapeutic Uses

Cathedral crystal absorbs vibrations and can help us open the chakras. When it is placed on a particular chakra, you will quickly get a feeling of incomparable gentleness. However, this gentleness shouldn't fool you—this stone is an electrical battery. If you leave it there for 20 minutes, it will fill you with energy. In some cases, its euphoric, bracing effect can cause slight insomnia. In that case, jade will help you to sleep well again. Although it acts on all the chakras, this crystal is partial to the heart chakra. It strengthens the myocardium and activates circulation.

Zodiac Correspondences

As with rock crystal, Capricorn's famous stubbornness will be reduced. Leo's need for power, which is often painful for others, will subside. Gemini will become more tolerant.

When its main tip is pointed toward the constellation of your zodiac sign, its beneficial effect is increased.

CRYSTAL:
HERKIMER CRYSTAL

Chemical composition: Silicon dioxide; a very shiny variety of rock crystal with several tips

Color: Transparent or milky white

Principal deposits: Mainly Herkimer County, New York

Hardness: 7

Density: 2.65

Etymology and General Characteristics

This beautiful rock crystal owes its name to Herkimer County, New York, the principal place where it is found. The stone is also called the "Herkimer diamond."

This stone symbolizes the balance between the sky and the earth, between the spirit and the body. It strengthens the influence of the other stones.

Therapeutic Uses

Herkimer crystal is the supreme remedy for fighting pain. The stone should be placed on the area that is hurting. After 3 or 4 minutes, the energetic current will start to circulate. The painful sensation is first reduced and then it disappears.

Zodiac Correspondences

As with rock crystal, Capricorn's famous stubbornness will be reduced. Leo's need for power, which is often painful to others, will subside. Gemini will become more tolerant.

CRYSTAL: PHANTOM CRYSTAL

Chemical composition: Silicon dioxide

Colors: White, gray, or light beige

Principal deposits: France (Alps), Madagascar, United States (Arkansas), Russia (Ural Mountains), and Brazil

Hardness: 7

Density: 2.65

Etymology and General Characteristics

Incomplete crystals, generally triangular in shape, are formed during the millions of years needed for quartz growth. These crystals stopped growing for several hundred millennia but started up again under the influence of the geological environment—the pressure, gas, and temperature. These "phantoms" represent these stones' history. This stone encourages meditation, introspection, and making peace with our past.

Therapeutic Uses

It has the same effects as rock crystal, with this exception: it is always beneficial. If you don't feel in harmony with this stone to begin with, you may have an uneasy feeling for several days, but this will dissipate in less than a week. You may also notice a redness of the skin that will quickly disappear. These psychosomatic effects show us that this is a "psychological" stone. It helps to heal anxiety and depression. By applying it on the Visuddha (fifth) chakra, on the Ajna (sixth) chakra, or even the Sahasrara (seventh) chakra, we can noticeably improve our problems with communication, clairvoyance, and balance.

Zodiac Correspondences

Phantom crystal corrects Saturn's often depressing influence. You can also use this stone if you are sensitive to the effects of the full moon.

CRYSTAL: RAINBOW CRYSTAL

Chemical composition: Silicon dioxide

Color: Transparent or milky white

Principal deposits: France (Alps), Madagascar, United States (Arkansas), Russia (Ural Mountains), and Brazil

Hardness: 7

Density: 2.65

Etymology and General Characteristics

This stone is also called "iris" or "laser quartz." When large in size, these stones preserve traces of the slow crystallization called "frost growth." Some of them act like prisms and reflect all the colors of the rainbow. These are diurnal stones to be used in full daylight.

Therapeutic Uses

In addition to sharing the effects of the other rock crystals, this stone is the best remedy for eliminating the scars caused by surgery or wounds. Its pure, dense light helps "knit" the skin together and also helps to heal sunburn, cuts, and acne. The focused energy of the rainbow crystal allows it to pinpoint its light to heal a specific area.

Zodiac Correspondences

As with rock crystal, Capricorn's famous stubbornness will be reduced, Leo's need for power will subside, and Gemini will become more tolerant.

CRYSTAL: ROCK CRYSTAL

Chemical composition: Pure silicon dioxide

Color: Transparent or milky white

Principal deposits: France (Alps), Madagascar, United States (Arkansas), Russia (Ural Mountains), and Brazil

Hardness: 7

Density: 2.65

Etymology and General Characteristics

Krystallos means "ice" in Greek and the rock crystal's light does appear cold. It is a stone of light, an ideal prism. It diffuses all the colors of the spectrum. Its dazzling clarity encourages purity, and it brings strength and clarity to our intellect.

The hypnotic quality of this stone is conducive for sleep, and it helps us to understand our dreams. It is also the stone of death; many cultures include it in their funeral rites.

Rock crystal is a protective stone, but with this mineral comes a certain responsibility. In fact, to benefit from its blessings, you have to feel in harmony with it—and deserve its gifts. Its purity can be intransigent.

It is rare to find someone who will benefit from a completely transparent rock crystal. We must find a rock crystal suitable to our state of inner purity. A milky white crystal is very effective and more suited to someone with feelings of guilt or other internal conflict.

True crystal balls are expensive and best left to experienced, professional seers.

Therapeutic Uses

This stone has many possible uses. Applying a rock crystal on a painful or injured area will purify it and relieve the pain. For blisters, crystal is used like a magnifying glass, by concentrating sunlight on the dead skin. The cut crystal will always emit its power in the direction of the tip. Aim or place the tip on the area to be healed. Polished crystals can be used for massages. It is also beneficial to have a few varieties of crystal.

Rock crystal cures diarrhea and is effective in stopping motion sickness. This stone relieved the migraine headaches that accompanied the visions of the German mystic Hildegard of Bingen. Her eyes, weary from gazing at the wonders she later described, recovered their visual acuity thanks to rock crystal. In this case, it was used in the form of water.

Rock crystal water is prepared during the night by soaking a crystal for eight hours in three quarts of distilled water. Never use spring or mineral water, the presence of other minerals, even in tiny quantities, will harm the rock crystal's action. Water prepared in this way during a full moon is even more effective.

Alcohol-tinged rock crystal is prescribed by some healers. This is 70 percent medicinal alcohol in which a crystal fragment has been left to soak during the night of a full moon. For depression, anxiety, or mourning, take one to three drops on a sugar cube three times a day. This preparation is also effective for a host of infections but it should be prescribed by a competent healer.

Rock crystal can also be used as a "catalyst." When allied with a bigger stone, its effects will be greatly improved.

Zodiac Correspondences

Capricorn's famous stubbornness will be reduced. Leo's need for power, which is often painful for others, will subside. Gemini will become more tolerant.

CRYSTAL: SCEPTER CRYSTAL

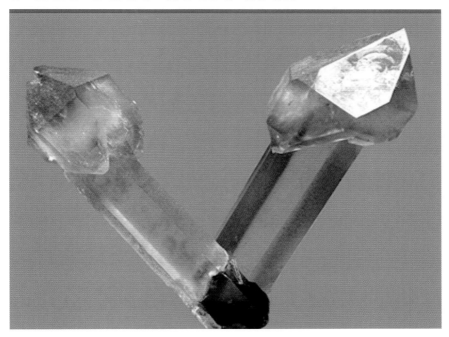

Chemical composition: Silicon dioxide

Color: White, beige, or gray

Principal deposits: France (Alps), Madagascar, United States (Arkansas), Russia (Ural Mountains), and Brazil

Hardness: 7

Density: 2.65

Etymology and General Characteristics

These crystals are only different from rock crystal by their special shape. Their tips are bulbous and opaque. The scepter crystal looks like two different stones stuck together—resembling a mushroom or the male organ. This is nature's way of symbolizing its essential nature: this masculine, virile stone can be used as a tool of domination and power.

It is also possible to make use of the positive aspects of this stone for self-healing.

Therapeutic Uses

Besides the effects common to all quartz stones, this stone is used to resolve sexual problems in both men and women. Given its power, it should be applied only for a short time. This stone can be dangerous and it's best to follow the advice of an experienced practitioner. When used correctly, there's nothing better to heal impotence and a low libido. But this stone should never be applied directly on the Svadhisthana (second) chakra. Anyone using this stone should be aware of the risk of sexual addiction.

A scepter crystal should be avoided by anyone who occupies a position of leadership. It could increase the tendency to persecute subordinates and may even lead to harassment, dictatorial behavior, and violence.

Again, this dangerous stone should only be used by a professional lithotherapist. It is necessary to be in harmony with this stone, otherwise it can present the same negative effects as ordinary rock crystal. If you appreciate this stone, it may be better to use it only as a decorative element in an entryway or bedroom.

Zodiac Correspondences

Those born under the signs of Virgo, Aquarius, Leo, Capricorn, and Scorpio should not use this crystal. Cancer can use scepter crystal moderately, but only under the direction of an experienced lithotherapist.

DIAMOND

Chemical composition: Crystallized carbon

Color: This stone is usually transparent but it can also be green, brown, blue, black, yellow, or, more rarely, pink.

Principal deposits: South Africa and central Africa, India, Brazil, Australia, and Russia (Siberia)

Hardness: 10

Density: 3.5

Etymology and General Characteristics

From the Greek *adamas,* which means "untamable," and *diaphanus,* meaning "transparent." The diamond is the only stone composed of a single element. In its uncut condition, it looks like any other pebble. Once it has been cut, even the tiniest stone looks sumptuous. The diamond is a friend of humanity; one reveals the other and vice versa.

The diamond symbolizes perfection, illumination—even ecstasy. It also represents divine love.

This stone gives us vitality and encourages us toward purity. According to the German mystic Hildegard of Bingen, sucking on a diamond will keep one from lying; it will also fool hunger, which makes fasting easier. Its huge market value is equal to its spiritual power.

Paradoxically, a diamond is the ideal stone for the ascetic who has given up on material wealth. It is the ideal object for diligent contemplation and deep meditation. The fact that it must be cut to reveal its beauty equates to the inner, spiritual beauty of the human being.

The cutting also symbolizes our resistance to challenges and adversity. It also corresponds to the cutting of fruit trees to make them produce the best fruit.

Therapeutic Uses

There's no need to own a high priced diamond. The tiniest little diamond will be effective—as much so as all the Crown's diamonds.

Diamonds combat the aging of the cells and strengthen vital energy. They cure constipation, urine retention, and in general, all organs concerned with removing waste from the body. Applying a diamond at the kidneys will accelerate the evacuation of stones. Do not leave a diamond on the abdomen too long. It's best to proceed in short sessions of 5 minutes. The effect will persist after it has been removed from the area. Jewelry can be safely worn on the hands and chest. Its power can become bothersome if it is worn at the navel level: watch out for this type of jewelry, especially if it is accompanied by gold.

The diamond is very beneficial for epileptics. It should be avoided in cases of paranoid psychosis, depressive manias, and obsessive jealousy. As a general rule, diamonds correspond to people who have worked on themselves. Given its purity, as with rock crystal, it can actually harm nasty individuals dominated by crude appetites. Too often, greedy, rich people who have acquired expensive diamonds have experienced the consequences of their actions. This has led to the belief that diamonds, or at least some of them, are "bad luck charms." Nothing could be farther from the truth; the so-called curse is only the result of the misalliance of an individual's low-level mental state with this symbol of purity and grandeur.

Zodiac Correspondences

The diamond corresponds to the most animal of the signs: Aries, Taurus, Capricorn, and Leo. The diamond is an especially good fit for the royal lion.

EMERALD

Chemical composition: Beryllium and aluminum silicate

Color: Dark green and yellow-green

Principal deposits: Russia (Ural Mountains), Pakistan, Colombia, South Africa, Brazil, and India

Hardness: 7.5 to 8

Density: 2.8

Etymology and General Characteristic

This stone's name comes from the Greek *smaragdos,* which means "green stone." Transparent, pure emerald is a precious stone. The translucent, opaque varieties are just as effective. This remarkable stone balances the spirit with the body, the emotions with the intellect. It symbolizes growth and hopes for the future. Emeralds also relieve emotional suffering. According to Hildegard of Bingen, the most knowledgeable of lithologists, all the green of nature is concentrated within the emerald.

The emerald's splendor, strength, and purity have an invigorating effect on thought, reflection, and philosophy. A Christian grammarian, a monk intoxicated with "the perfume of grammar," once chose the name Smaragde to place himself under the protection of this stone so as to better write lucid, scholarly treatises. The emerald no doubt served him; this polished stone was also used as a magnifying glass, which enabled him to read even when his eyes were tiring.

The emerald was once called *beryl,* like many other stones in its family. Those that were polished so that people could see better through them were called *bericles.* The linguistic evolution gave us the French word *besicles,* which then designated the very first eyeglasses.

The "goddess of the precious stones," the emerald vivifies and activates artistic creativity. It is also the symbol of a certain kind of innocence, purity without naïveté, an honesty that is not unfamiliar with the baseness of the world. That is why Victor Hugo placed under its protection the lively Esmeralda, the gypsy dancer wrongly tortured in Notre Dame de Paris.

Therapeutic Uses

A stone of youth, the emerald combats aging. By placing it over tired organs, one gets a revitalizing effect. But beyond its ability to be cut into a magnifying glass or used as glasses, the emerald enhances vision; the Egyptians of the High Empire used it for this purpose. The Greeks and the Romans stuck small emeralds in the corners of the eyes of nearsighted or farsighted people. The emerald's regenerative aspect is shown once again as farsightedness is mainly an ailment of aging.

An emerald gemstone worn as a pendant has a good effect on vision in and of itself. If you put one or two little emeralds in the sidepieces of a pair of eyeglasses, you will surprise yourself by putting down the glasses while you read with the naked eye. Eye baths of emerald water will also be effective (let an emerald soak for one night in demineralized water).

Drinking emerald water soothes gas and cardiac weaknesses. It is an excellent stimulant in treating gout. In addition, it can strengthen memory.

A jewel comprising emerald and rock crystal has a significant balancing effect.

Zodiac Correspondences

Emerald will nurture the innate spirituality of the Taurus native and help him symbolically to "see things clearly." This stone will have an invigorating effect on the often indecisive Cancer. The emerald will encourage meditation and reflection in those born under the sign of Capricorn.

FLUORITE

Chemical composition: Of the halogenous family; calcium fluoride also called fluorine

Color: This soft feldspar can be colorless, yellow, orange, red, black, green, purple, or blue. The same stone can contain several of these shades.

Principal deposits: Germany, Switzerland, France, Spain, England, and South Africa

Hardness: 4

Density: 3.1

Etymology and General Characteristics

Fluorite owes its name to the fluorine it contains. Fluorine comes from the Latin *fluere,* "to flow." Like chrysocolla, fluorite was used in metallurgy to fluidify metals. Having a crystalline, cubic structure, fluorite doesn't appear natural. It actually looks as if it was artificially

produced. This stone hasn't finished its evolution. As a result, it favors new projects and strengthens patience, and it speeds up the processes of healing.

Fluorite is called the "stone of the genius," and it helps us to "think on our feet." It symbolizes the one who thinks—calmly or with boiling intensity. It stimulates both scholars and poets and it can even boost the IQ. Fluorite is truly a stone for the twenty-first century. It harmonizes with computer technology, information processing, and scientific research. All you need to do is hold it in your hand to feel its surprising effects.

The color of the stone also affects its particular qualities. (See chapter 6, The Language of Colors.)

Therapeutic Uses

Fluorite deepens meditation and relieves mental disturbances. The distortions in personality, intelligence, and character that are often linked are healed if this stone is worn day and night for several months. This stone can help us discover our true potential. Thanks to this stone, many people have changed directions and started new, more successful careers.

Zodiac Correspondences

Always a beneficial stone, purple fluorite is particularly favorable for Pisces. Its earthy stability will help them complete their projects. The blue, or light blue variety, will help those born under the sign of Aquarius to think more creatively.

GARNET

Chemical composition: Magnesium and aluminum double silicate

Color: Red garnet is the best known but there are also orange, brown, and purple stones.

Principal deposits: Sri Lanka, India, Brazil, Sweden, Norway, United States (Alaska, Arizona), Afghanistan, South Africa, and Australia

Hardness: 7 to 7.5

Density: 4.5

Etymology and General Characteristics

From the Sanskrit *gar,* "to transport," or from the Greek *gêron,* "old," and *granum,* a Latin word meaning "seed" or "that which has several seeds." The word *pomegranate* stems from the latter and it is from the fruit that the name of the stone evolved, probably stemming from the similarity in color.

Garnet represents the primordial fire, the creation of the world out of chaos, purification, and love—but also hatred and jealousy. It is the stone of strong, intense feelings.

The varieties of garnet bear different technical names based on their color: pyrope for red; almandine for the brown and opaque stones; and grossulaire, uvaorite, and melanite for the brown stones that are almost black. The pyrope variety owes its color to its strong concentration of magnesium and aluminum. The almandine stone is ferrous and aluminum-like with traces of manganese and/or magnesium.

A warrior's stone, garnet served as a talisman in the Crusades for both the Christians and their Muslim enemies. The Merovingians brought garnets from faraway Ceylon (Sri Lanka) through the Silk Road. They combined it with amber from the Baltic to create their magnificent jewels. These two stones, one warm, the other cold, balanced each other. Some see the source of the Frankish civilization in this combination, since the amber would have tempered the warrior-like fieriness of the Germanic people.

Therapeutic Uses

Infected wounds, acne, depression, disturbances in the cardiac rhythm (except for arterial hypertension, which garnet can even aggravate), and low libido can all be alleviated with garnet.

The other sexual disorders are also relieved by applying a garnet directly to the genital organs. Princess Palatine discovered her husband, the brother of King Louis XIV, applying garnets on his body in this way. He asked her not to tell anyone. Instead, she told the whole court and wrote about it in her many famous letters.

Garnets relieve rheumatic and arthritic pain and some psychological illnesses. It also helps widows to find a new husband! It not only calms sadness and emotional pain, it also helps those who have gone through great despair to get back on their feet. The garnet has helped widows who have mourned for too long to regain their spirit and become seductive again. The same is no doubt true for widowers as well. This stone will also soothe us when we're disappointed by love.

Zodiac Correspondences

The garnet is a conqueror's stone. Legend has it that a garnet ornamented Don Juan's ring. The strong, sexy signs—Leo, Aries, and Scorpio—will make the best use of this stone.

GEM SALT

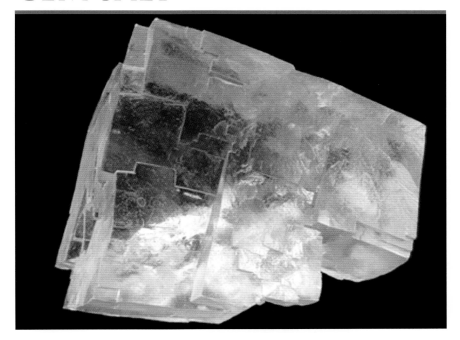

Chemical composition: Sodium chloride

Color: Transparent and translucent with a glassy brilliance; this mineral constitutes a crystalline crust.

Principal deposits: Egypt (Wadi Natrum), Gobi Desert, and Italy (Sicily)

Hardness: 2

Density: 2.1

Etymology and General Characteristics

From the Latin *sal,* gem salt or rock salt is often richer in certain trace elements than sea salt. It presents a telluric force and has long been considered a sacred element. It is the origin of the word salary, for it once served as a means of payment—a bargaining chip or currency. Salt is a purifying substance. Christ's spokesman, in the Gospel according to

Saint Matthew, is "the salt of the earth." Salt is shared like bread. It is the food of fraternity and friendship. It represents solidity through its crystallization.

Its antiseptic proprieties make it a symbol of incorruptibility. It combats decay and preserves food. It evokes longevity or eternity—but also sterility and aridity. The water of bitterness, the bitter chalice, is the burning salt one must drink on the day of Revelation. Since the beginning of time, hermits have retreated to the great salt deserts—like Wadi Natrum in Egypt—to live alone in the permanent celebration of the divine, the quest for meaning and God.

Salt crystal is very decorative and often used for lamps. Its ionizing presence is conducive to relaxation. It tempers the great quantity of positive ions generated by our electrical apparatuses—computers, telephones, and microwave ovens. It restores the joy of living and drives away bad moods.

Therapeutic Uses

Salt is toxic in its pure state. Too much salt in our diet can cause a variety of health ailments. Salt enhances water retention, which saturates the tissues and encourages weight gain. Cutting back on salt is a must for anyone with cardiac problems. Too much salt can also have a psychological effect. It exacerbates the problems of low libido and depression. But salt in crystal form, placed on the skin, can have beneficial effects. It can direct organic currents toward a painful spot.

In case of fever, let several salt crystals melt on your chest over your heart. The slight irritation to the skin is a small price to pay for the immediate relief it brings. Putting salt at the corners of the lips helps salivation.

Zodiac Correspondences

Salt brings wisdom to those born under the signs of Capricorn and Aquarius. Gem Salt will help Libras to face the harsh realities of life.

HELIOTROPE

Chemical composition: Aluminum and magnesium double silicate

Color: This quartz contains iron, which gives it a dark green hue spotted with red.

Principal deposits: France, Egypt, United States, and Russia

Hardness: 7

Density: 2.5 to 2.8

Etymology and General Characteristics

Heliotrope comes from the Greek *helios,* meaning "sun," and *trepein,* "to attract." It is also the botanical name for the oleaginous plant called the sunflower. The red spots that contrast with the beautiful green color of this stone have given it the name "bloodstone." It is also called "Christ's stone"—as Christ is considered by some to be the Sun God. The red spots were compared to the blood flowing from his seven wounds.

Heliotrope fortifies the body. It can "overexcite" it after a period of convalescence. The combination of the green and red focuses the healing radiance toward the organs used to eliminate bodily wastes. It also focuses on the elimination of toxins through the pores of the skin.

Therapeutic Uses

Heliotrope purifies and fortifies the blood. It is a powerful hemostat to be used during the change of seasons—especially at the end of winter. It can help you to avoid many types of anemia. Heliotrope in powder form was once used in a variety of antidotes.

Heliotrope plunged into cold water stops nosebleeds. Massage the bridge of the nose for 5 to 6 minutes. The stone should stay wet; dunk it back into the water as many times as necessary. Heliotrope also relieves mosquito bites. The intestines and liver will be relieved by applying this stone to the stomach. Heliotrope water relieves varicose veins and hemorrhoids. It also restores self-confidence and soothes the inferiority complexes that handicap many people.

Zodiac Correspondences

This stone will reduce the aggressiveness of those born under the signs of Aries and Scorpio.

HEMATITE

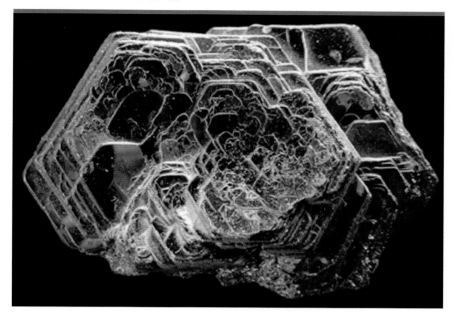

Chemical composition: Iron sesquioxide

Color: Hematite looks like iron and can be found in a black, gray, or brownish red color. It is always opaque.

Principal deposits: The Alps, Germany, Italy, Russia (Ural Mountains), Sweden, Australia, Great Britain, Switzerland, and Brazil

Hardness: 5.5 to 6.3

Density: 5.2 to 5.3

Etymology and General Characteristics

Hematite owes its name to the Greek *hematos,* which means "blood." When cut, it will turn water red. Hematite is also called "sanguine" and "specular iron."

With its metallic brilliance, this stone was used to make mirrors in antiquity. It is the origin of the term "specular iron" from the Latin *speculum,* meaning "mirror." Hematite also served as a "prophetic" mirror; fortune-tellers once used it to see the future. The Oriental tradition claims it is favorable for premonitory dreams.

This energizing stone makes people feel joyful. It is a good stone for mischievous spirits. It drives out gloomy thoughts. It is also a good stone for those who listen to others, whether by inclination or profession: it tempers judgment and encourages kindness. It also strengthens determination, will power, and wisdom. Although it is classified among the red stones, it does not have the disquieting or dangerous aspects that most of them have.

Therapeutic Uses

Hematite fights anemia and problems of the blood and the lymph glands. It should be applied to the heart or lungs. Placed on a wound, it stops the bleeding.

Hematite is the best remedy for cardiac arrhythmia. It regulates the flow of bile. It also has a slight effect in the treatment of thrombosis (blood clots). It is effective for skin ulcers. In cases of stiffness of the neck or cramps in the bottom of the feet, hematite will be soothing while you wait for magnesium vitamins to eliminate this excess of lactic acid. The blood-colored water, made by rubbing hematite in demineralized water, is an excellent energizer. It was once one of the ingredients for an iron liqueur along with steel nails and mercury—all of it stewed in alcohol. The presence of mercury obviously makes this "remedy" far more harmful than the disorders it was purported to cure.

Finally, placed under the pillow, this stone will bring refreshing sleep without nightmares.

Zodiac Correspondences

Hematite will drive out the gloomy thoughts of those born under the sign of Scorpio. This stone's metallic brilliance is in tune with the Aries spirit; it will strengthen the determination of the Aries native, and help him to fulfill his ambitions.

IOLITE

Chemical composition: An aluminosilicate of magnesium and iron

Color: Blue, mauve, or purple

Principal deposits: Madagascar, Sri Lanka, Brazil, India, Thailand, and Myanmar (Burma)

Hardness: 7 to 7.5

Density: 3.3

Etymology and General Characteristics

Iolite gets its name from the violet, a flower whose name is *ios* in Greek. Its other name, *cordiérite,* gives homage to the French mineralogist P. Cordier. This stone evokes the Scandinavia of the Vikings. Strips of iolite were used as a navigation tool, which made their far-off explorations possible. Iolite changes colors from one side to the other. One side will seem transparent, another the color of honey, a third a mauvish blue. This particularity is called "dichroism," the origin of the word *dichroite,* which was once applied to this stone.

Therapeutic Uses

This stone enhances our spiritual aspirations. Iolite also orients and helps us to recover our balance. Because of this, it is recommended for people suffering from disorientation, lack of motivation, chronic disorganization, and distraction.

It regularizes digestion and enhances hair and nail growth. Iolite can also be used for sore throats.

Zodiac Correspondences

Pisces will be calmed by iolite's lively colors. It will help Aries to think more creatively.

JADE

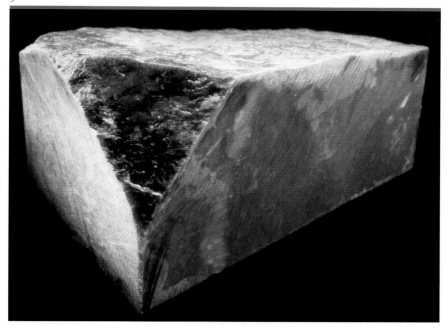

Chemical composition: Aluminum and sodium double silicate

Color: This stone can present a great number of colors and subtle shades such as green, red, yellow, purple, grayish black, or mauve.

Principal deposits: Myanmar (Burma), China, Japan, Tibet, Mexico, and Peru. Some deposits are also found in Greece and Italy.

Hardness: 6 to 7

Density: 3.2 to 3.4

Etymology and General Characteristics

Jade is often confused with nephrite; the same word designated both stones in ancient China. Jade, said to be an "emblem of perfection," is associated with many great cultures. The Spanish, who used it for meditation and prayer, called it *Piedra de ijada* when they conquered the New World. This word remains, distorted, in our language.

The Incas and the Aztecs used jade or obsidian knives to tear out the hearts of the human sacrifices they offered to make the rebirth of the sun and rain god possible. Jade, under the name "precious water," symbolized the blood spilled in this ritual.

Jade is also beloved by both China and Korea ("country of the calm morning"), two great kingdoms that date back for millennia. Like Asia itself, jade is calm and bubbling, cruel and compassionate, wise and full of temper, intoxicated with both war and opium. This stone represents contrasts that are balanced at the price of crises. Because of this, jade has helped both leaders and common people bear adversity during great political conflicts. The jade Buddha is a symbol of calm strength. It represents serenity in the middle of storms.

Jade also represents justice and honesty. This does not prevent many Chinese businessmen—or the members of the Japanese mob—from keeping a piece of it in their pockets. In the past, both religious leaders and the cruelest chiefs of war used jade to calm themselves and to confront their destiny. They used jade as a symbol representing both sides of the coin. It is the stone of the saint and the bandit, the monk and the assassin. It is the stone of kamikazes of the "divine wind," those who sacrificed themselves serenely for their country while trying, at the same time, to kill the maximum number of enemies. Thus, jade is in harmony both with the great warlike conflicts, as well as our internal conflicts and intimate problems. It is also a kindly stone, one that represents compassion, forgiveness, and understanding.

Therapeutic Uses

As a general rule, jade is the stone of calm in the midst of the storm. Its action balances nerves and cardiac rhythm. Jade is also the stone of the flank and the kidneys. It heals kidney and bladder illnesses.

Putting a jade fragment in the hand of a woman giving birth—or better yet, a small jade sculpture representing the female sex organs—will help with a difficult childbirth. Jade can also be used for teenage girls with anorexia, and for mothers who are afraid of not knowing how to parent their children.

Jade helps reduce the symptoms of several disorders: shingles, herpes, some eczemas, burning and itching without specific skin problems, morning insomnia, selective memory, genital mycoses, and candida. It is also used to treat the flu.

Jade heals migraines, according to Hildegard of Bingen, who in the tenth century had horrendous migraines that brought on her famous visions. In one vision, she "saw" all the qualities of the stones—the subject of a hallucinated treatise. For migraine relief, place the stone on your forehead and breathe deeply.

Jade does an excellent job of healing feelings of guilt. It will also be very beneficial in extreme cases of defeatism or "pathological normality," that is, an excessive desire to adapt oneself to a group even if it is sectlike conformity, exaggerated militarism, a follow-the-leader attitude (the irrepressible need to follow fashion), or the compulsive desire to acquiesce to the general opinion to integrate oneself into a group whatever the cost.

It is a good idea to keep a fragment of jade in your pocket—or in a pendant—to stroke from time to time to recharge your energy.

Zodiac Correspondences

Jade has an affinity with the signs of Libra, Pisces, and Cancer. It will give those born under these signs a feeling of calm strength and serenity in the midst of an emotional storm.

JASPER

Chemical composition: Silicon dioxide

Color: This is a kind of quartz with large granulation. Jasper can be found in all colors. It is almost always spotted, speckled, striped, or iridescent.

Principal deposits: France, India, Egypt, the Americas, Russia, and the African continent

Hardness: 6.5 to 7

Density: 2.5 to 2.8

Etymology and General Characteristics

From the Greek *iaspis,* meaning "agate." Jasper was once considered "the mother of stones." In many ancient civilizations, it was thought to be heavily charged with mysterious and sometimes contradictory properties. People wore it to protect themselves from eye problems and to remain lucid. Red jasper stimulates without being excessive.

Yellow jasper enhances common sense but also conformity. In some cases, it can make one sententious. Green jasper that is all of one color harmonizes gently; it can change the opinion of even the most stubborn person. Green jasper spotted with red has special qualities (see Heliotrope). Multicolor jasper has the qualities of its dominant color, without neglecting those of the other colors.

Jasper creates a special aura, something primordial that is hard to explain but easily felt by holding the stone in your hand. Its irradiation throughout the body is a very pleasant sensation for people who know how to be sensitive to its vibration. The calm feeling produced can make us feel generous, even humble. We feel full of compassion and patience. It is also a symbol of giving birth.

In the Apocalypse, Saint John sees the Eternal appear on a throne of jasper or carnelian; the jasper represents eternal youth, renewal, and revelation. Some fortune-tellers used jasper as part of their divination ritual. In ancient and medieval traditions, jasper was the stone of the "tempestaries," magical masters of the wind and rain. They were called upon in secret to save the harvests in periods of drought, or to save the ships from storms. Their services cost a great deal, sometimes even damnation.

Everything in jasper is seen as potential—the light that strengthens our inner clarity is not yet seen. This ordinary "pebble" hasn't yet delivered all its secrets. Yet, in its common aspect, it fascinates, intrigues—and heals.

Therapeutic Uses

Jasper soothes epilepsy and heals gout. In cases of blood problems (particularly anemia), move a piece of jasper over your veins. Never use a tourniquet. Kidney stones will be reduced in a few days by treating them with jasper. Digestive problems will be soothed with jasper water (let the stone soak in demineralized water overnight). Jasper strengthens the stomach, enhances digestion, and calms nausea and vomiting. It also stops nosebleeds and reduces hemorrhoids.

Jasper protects people from bewitchment. It is conducive to happy pregnancies. It is also a powerful aphrodisiac and a regenerator of sperm, especially when it is combined with garnet or topaz. Jasper amulets in the form of a penis have been found in many ancient civilizations.

Zodiac Correspondences

This stone will give Cancer and Capricorn compassion and patience. Aries and Scorpio will benefit from any type of jasper but red jasper will help those born under the sign of Aries to calm their hot tempers. Aries and Scorpio are also especially drawn to the heliotrope variety. Red Jasper will give Virgo natives the strength and persistence they need to achieve their goals.

JET

Chemical composition: Fossil lignite

Color: Shiny black

Principal deposits: Baltic Sea, England (Yorkshire), France, Spain (Asturies, Aragon, Souable), Poland, and Vietnam

Hardness: 2.5 to 4

Density: 1.30 to 1.35

Etymology and General Characteristics

Old French gives the word *gayet,* or *jayet,* a form that is still found in Swiss Romande, the French speaking part of Switzerland.

Jet is cut in facets to make various ornaments, jewels, bishop's crooks, and other liturgical or mourning objects. In the nineteenth century, jet was used to make beautiful jewels that were thought to bring good luck. The Egyptians, Hindus, and Romans used jet for amulets to protect themselves from the evil eye. The Celts believed that jet drove away demons and conjured up the Fates. They also used it as an antidote. In Ireland, women used to burn jet (it's a very flammable coal) to ensure the safety and fidelity of their husbands when they were at sea or war. In the eleventh century, a French bishop named Marbode wrote that touching the vaginal secretions of a young girl with a jet fragment could verify her virginity: if the fragment dissolved, she was no longer a virgin. Jet is also called "black amber" due to its electrical properties.

Therapeutic Uses

Jet is apparently the best pharmaceutical coal to be used for gas and other digestive problems. A jet powder concoction, according to Marbode, will give a woman back her period. Applying a jet stone to a woman's stomach will make her menstrual flow regular, which can activate her fertility. By rubbing it on a wool cloth, you can use jet as you would amber; you can also use it in combination with that stone. This combination is very powerful and can cure the pain of rheumatism and lumbago. Since it fights stomach ailments, jet was once used as an antidote for poisons such as arsenic. It's a protective stone for overall good health.

Zodiac Correspondences

Jet has an affinity with the feminine sign of Cancer. It is also a good stone for Virgo. Jet's calm vibration will help those born under the sign of Scorpio to balance their volatile moods. Gemini and Pisces natives can also benefit from jet if it is used with amber. These two stones are "sisters."

KUNZITE

Chemical composition: Lithium aluminum silicate

Color: A stone of beautiful, glassy transparency, its color goes from pale pink to light purple according to the angle of observation

Principal deposits: Afghanistan, Brazil, Madagascar, and North America

Hardness: 6 to 7

Density: 3.2 to 3.5

Etymology and General Characteristics

Kunzite owes its name to the mineralogist G. F. Kunz who discovered it at the beginning of the twentieth century. The purple represents the elevation of mind—as with amethyst—combined with the tender, light pink of love.

This is a linking stone, a stone of mediation between heaven and earth. This stone encourages us to go right toward the essential, the absolute—so much so that it can make our everyday life seem devoid of meaning. It is also often associated with more earthly stones: jet, jasper, and hematite. The need to be grounded is the reason that the most "exalted" monks are given the most banal, commonplace tasks to balance their spiritual aspirations. Spiritual lucidity joined with a love that is too ungrounded can lead to difficulty. So we must approach this stone with precision and determination, knowing exactly what it is that we want.

Adopting such a stone as a companion, as a pendant or a ring, requires understanding. Its parallel streaks can create structure, but this stone can also produce too strong a will for the rigor and purity it can inspire in us. We must make sure our thinking doesn't become too linear to enjoy the blessings that this stone can bring. Kunzite will lead us toward a perfect spiritual and emotional elevation, or close to it, as long as tenderness and compassion are mixed in.

Therapeutic Uses

Kunzite was neglected for a long time. People thought it did the same job as other stones. It's only recently that its very special qualities, both powerful and subtle, have been discovered. The stone's "personality" has not yet been well explored. Research is still underway.

However, it has already been shown that it can help people who have been disappointed in love, whose purity has been ridiculed, making them susceptible to cardiovascular problems. Kunzite gently energizes the heart's mechanical rhythm. It makes it possible to gradually reestablish a rhythm harmonized with the breath. From that point, the body's blood circulation will balance the mind and body.

Zodiac Correspondences

Problems of blood circulation are common in Libras. The calming effect of kunzite will help those born under this sign to feel more secure.

Pisces sometimes lacks a sense of reality. It was once believed that kunzite would not be beneficial for this sign. And yet, paradoxically, it is. This stone, which can elevate us to the highest spheres, can help Pisces to keep their feet on the ground. Their tendency to be ungrounded cancels out the effects of this stone, which produces a powerful balancing effect.

LABRADORITE

Chemical composition: Sodium and calcium alumino-silicate

Color: Deep gray to yellowish black, blue, and red; the brilliant colors of this feldspar are referred to as "labradorization"

Principal deposits: Canada (Labrador, Newfoundland), Mexico, Russia (Ural Mountains), and North and Central America

Hardness: 6 to 6.5

Density: 2.6

Etymology and General Characteristics

This stone was discovered in Labrador in 1770. In 1940, a particularly colorful stone was discovered in Ylijärvi, in Carelia, Finland. It was named spectrolite, as it reflected all the colors in the spectrum. However, it was later discovered to be just a superb variety of labradorite.

Sometimes labradorite doesn't look like much: You will only discover its beauty by examining it closely. But when you do, you'll be fascinated by its sparkling quality. Each stone has its own personality: a bit of intuition will enable you to choose the one that is suitable for you. The stone will give you a sign that it's the right one for you—it may even look like you!

This stone increases clairvoyant abilities and powers of perception. It helps develop clarity and the ability to see auras.

Therapeutic Uses

Labradorite can heal our depression and shame—the negative side of our personality that can saturate our being like a drug. In addition, this stone helps to detoxify the effects of tobacco, alcohol, and to a lesser extent, hard drugs.

Labradorite helps develop the hands' sensitivity. It is useful for the physiotherapist or healer.

Zodiac Correspondences

The Pisces people will especially appreciate the red stone: it will give them spectacular energy. The yellow stone will give them a vital warmth that sad people will be drawn to. It's important that Pisces not become overwhelmed by kindness and compassion. The green stone promotes inner peace in those suffering from cardiovascular or respiratory problems.

Cancer will savor the labradorite and should own several stones of different colors. The mauve stone will "heat up" the top of the skull—allowing the electromagnetic energy of the brain's thinking to be felt. Cancer will be able to feel the weight of his ideas as if they were material and concrete. This will help to break through the distorting mirror of illusion, make vague ideas specific, and realize dreams. Surprising results and shivers guaranteed! The yellow stone will enhance concentration. Be careful, the action that follows will astonish more than one person.

LAPIS LAZULI

Chemical composition: Aluminum and sodium sulfured silicate

Color: Sky or dark blue

Principal deposits: China, the area around Lake Baikal (Russia), Afghanistan, Myanmar (Burma), Thailand, Egypt, and South America

Hardness: 5 to 6

Density: 2.4 to 2.9

Etymology and General Characteristics

From the Latin and Spanish *lapis* and the Arabic *azul,* from which came the French word *azure.* A symbol of the starry night in ancient Persia and pre-Columbian America, lapis lazuli is the favorite stone in the Islamic Orient for those who want to protect themselves from the evil eye.

Its grainy structure can make it look velvety. The blue color doesn't appear cold, but soft, gentle, almost sensual. The dark varieties, with

their pyrite inclusions, look like "night fragments," pieces of the starry night sky. It is the "sky's stone" of the ancient Egyptians who often sculpted it in the form of good luck scarabs, which represented the sun's path. Lapis lazuli in its natural state doesn't look like much. It reveals its beauty only after it has been cut or polished. Lapis lazuli that has been ground up produces the intense, superb color used by Michelangelo. A very expensive color, it annoyed the patrons of this inspired painter who believed the stone was better used as a talisman.

Therapeutic Uses

Lapis lazuli enhances circulation, improves the cardiac rhythm, and regulates the secretions of the endocrine glands. It is a supremely effective remedy for skin problems and also relieves cramps, stiffness, and lumbago. When heated in sunlight, it reduces bruises and insect bites. In the past, it was used for jaundice in newborn babies and adults. Oozing or septic sties and other eye infections will be relieved by rubbing the infected zone with a fragment of lapis lazuli heated in warm water. Once the water has cooled down, it can be used in eye baths. Like many stones and remedies used for the eyes, lapis lazuli also heals problems regarding arterial tension.

As it represents the regularity of the planets' path and the passing of days, this stone is very effective for women suffering from menstrual irregularities. The ancient Egyptians likened it to Isis, the one who brings Osiris back, "puts things back in place," and restores the immutable cycles.

Zodiac Correspondences

Lapis lazuli is a good stone for those born under the sign of Sagittarius. It will expand their awareness of spiritual truths and calm their agitation.

The sun is in Virgo at the time of the harvests, which symbolizes fertility. Opposite and complementary, lapis lazuli and Virgo both represent time. Lapis lazuli's heavenly aspect will balance Virgo's earthly orientation.

This stone can also help Taurus develop the virtues of patience and perseverance.

MAGNESITE

Chemical composition: Magnesium carbonate

Color: Ivory-colored or colorless, may be tinted yellow or brown

Principal deposits: Turkey, Middle East, China, and United States (Arizona)

Hardness: 4

Density: 2.6

Etymology and General Characteristics

From the Greek *magnes,* meaning "magnet," this stone owes its name to the magnesium from which it's made. Magnesite is not very attractive.

By coloring it, some unscrupulous merchants "transform" it into turquoise. This deception still happens frequently.

Therapeutic Uses

This stone is called the "poor person's turquoise," since it possesses the powers of that stone in a very diminished way. Magnesite's primary application is in fighting obesity and helping with urinary elimination. Of course, its real weight-reduction power cannot manifest if one doesn't make at least a small effort at dieting. A little weight may be lost initially, but not much more until bad habits are changed. Cutting down the consumption of candy bars and sugary, carbonated drinks by even one-quarter will allow for real weight loss. Making this change and working with magnesite will also suppress the compulsive desire to overeat. The stone's ability to help in weight reduction is stimulated by combining it with a zirconium stone. Bulimia can be treated by combining magnesite with amber and chalcedony.

If ingested, the magnesium could help us get back into shape. But at this high dosage, it would be dangerous. It's better to opt for store-bought magnesium preparations or specific mineral waters.

Zodiac Correspondences

Those of turquoise, but in a very reduced way.

MAGNETITE

Chemical composition: Iron oxide

Color: Black or grayish, with occasional golden highlights

Principal deposits: Alps, Germany, Italy, Russia (Ural Mountains), Sweden, Australia, Great Britain, and Brazil

Hardness: 5.5 to 7

Density: 5.2 to 5.5

Etymology and General Characteristics

From the Greek *magnes,* which means "magnet." Magnetite is the stone of the North, which served for a long time as a rudimentary compass for the hardy navigators of the first centuries. The Greek philosopher Thales, in the sixth century BC, discovered static electricity (see Amber) as well as magnetism. The stone of lovers, magnetite represents cosmic attraction, as amber symbolizes the spiritual connection.

For the Egyptians, magnetism, connected to the god Horus, participated in regulating the cosmic movements. Magnetite looks like hematite but is often less shiny.

Therapeutic Uses

Magnetite, by reorienting the flow of energy in the body, fights pain—this is its main use. It's best to stick it on a painful place with honey that's been slightly concentrated by cooking. You can apply honey to the stone with a cotton ball, a handkerchief, or a bandage—as long as it's not made from synthetic fibers.

But be forewarned: sometimes, at the beginning of the treatment, magnetite accentuates certain pains. It should be used sparingly at first, about a half-hour to three-quarters of an hour per day. After two days, the stone will recover its analgesic effect following its intense, magnetic "discharge."

Never use magnetite if you are wearing a pacemaker or any other kind of cardiac stimulator; it could interfere with those devises. In the same way, wearing magnetite in a hospital can falsify the results of some tests.

Like rock crystal, magnetite strengthens the powers of the other stones. A stone of regularity, it will help make the menstrual cycle regular. Magnetite is a stone of the seeker. It will help those who are seeking the light, and those who are on a spiritual quest.

Zodiac Correspondences

Magnetite is suitable for the emotional intensity of Scorpio. It will help those born under this sign to channel their energy in a positive direction.

For Aries, magnetite will help reduce the tendency to dominate others. It will increase sensitivity and reduce feelings of jealousy.

MALACHITE

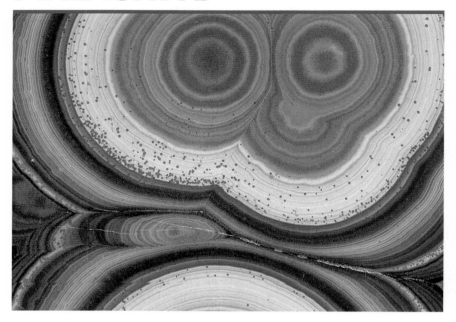

Chemical composition: Copper carbonate

Color: Light green to olive green; crystallized malachite can shine like aquamarine

Principal deposits: The African continent (Congo, Zimbabwe), United States (Arizona), Russia (Ural Mountains), Australia, Chile, and Peru

Hardness: 3.5 to 4

Density: 3.9

Etymology and General Characteristics

From the Greek *malachê,* meaning "mallow," in reference to the green leaves of the medicinal plant. This dull stone is porous and receptive. Malachite, combined with lapis lazuli and turquoise, was used by the Egyptians. They embellished this beautiful combination with copper.

Egyptian women also used it as eye shadow as we can see in the frescoes of the pyramids.

In addition to an aesthetic appreciation of these stones, the Egyptians also had a deep knowledge of their power. The combinations were balanced either by the proportions of each stone, or by the mystical power of the objects and the people represented.

In Switzerland and in several villages of Savoie in the French Alps, malachite crosses are thought to bring good luck to pregnant women. Mothers of large families are often proud to show their collections of malachite crosses. Collectors have crosses that date back to the fifteenth century. The most delicately crafted crosses belonged to women of high nobility.

Malachite is one of the stones dedicated to Saint Francis of Assisi. So great is this association that legend has it that malachite, held in the hand or worn as a jewel, will enable one to understand the language of animals. You might even be able to communicate with them if you regularly drink out of a cup cut from a block of this stone.

Therapeutic Uses

Malachite is a supremely effective remedy for female problems: it makes the menstrual cycle regular and eases labor.

Cold sweats, malaria, trembling, and Parkinson's disease are relieved, if not cured, by malachite. It can help people with asthma, but not as effectively as aquamarine. Intestinal problems are quickly relieved by malachite. During the Crimean war, when soldiers were suffering from cholera, local sorcerers sold them malachite powder at the price of gold to dilute in water. This remedy apparently kept the epidemic from spreading.

Copper treats rheumatic pain. In the form of basic carbonate— which is malachite—it has shown to be even more effective. An aid in elimination, this diuretic stone can help to cure kidney and gallstones. It fights osteoarthritis, especially that of the spine, and strengthens memory. It will help those who, suffering from short-term memory loss, forget the names of people right after hearing them. It will help grandparents who are worried about momentarily forgetting the names of their grandchildren—or confusing the generations.

Zodiac Correspondences

A stone of fertility, malachite will develop the creative potential of all the signs to various degrees.

The love that earthy Taurus feels for the natural world will be strengthened by wearing a ring ornamented with malachite. Scorpio's animal nature will be transformed into a productive creative force by malachite. The creativity unleashed in Cancer will be spectacular, especially for artists, painters, and musicians.

MEERSCHAUM

Chemical composition: Magnesium hydrosilicate

Color: White, sometimes bordering on yellow or gray

Principal deposits: Mainly in Eskischehir in Anatolia (Turkey), but also in South Africa

Hardness: 2

Density: 3

Etymology and General Characteristics

The German word *meerschaum* means "sea foam," and this mineral is sometimes referred to by that name. Some believe the name comes from the fact that this stone floats on water, due to its low density. This stone is also called sepiolite.

Meerschaum is the smoker's stone. It is used to make beautiful, sculpted pipes appreciated by tobacco connoisseurs. Some of these pipes are works of art shown in museum collections. Meerschaum diminishes the harmful effects of tobacco by absorbing the nicotine.

Therapeutic Uses

Meerschaum, pure magnesium reduced to powder form, was once used to heal gastric acidity. The foam, polished in spheres or in an egg shape, can be used to massage the stomach or the solar plexus in cases of pain or contractions. It relaxes the nape of the neck and momentarily relieves the pain of cervical osteoarthritis.

Zodiac Correspondences

An amulet cut in meerschaum that represents their sign or any other beloved object would be beneficial for Aquarians. Meerschaum will have a calming effect on both Cancers and Sagittarians.

MICA

Chemical composition: Potassium and aluminum

Color: Mica is translucent, in a glassy or pearly color of various shades.

Principal deposits: Brazil, Madagascar, Mozambique, United States (California), and Russia

Hardness: 2 to 2.5

Density: 2.7 to 3

Etymology and General Characteristics

Mica is a generic name for the phyllosilicates, a group that includes lepidolitus and muscovite. In everyday language, the word *mica* designates muscovite. This mineral appears in layers and gets its name from a deposit near the city of Moscow. In earlier times, mica was widely used in Russia to garnish windows.

Mica is flexible but nonelastic. Brittle and resistant to heat, it was once used as an electric insulator for wooden and coal frying pans.

Mica is a powerful good-luck stone. It attracts lasting success.

Therapeutic Uses

Mica protects the skin, nails, and hair, which can become dull through too much alcohol or tobacco and the stresses of modern life.

It is both a calming and exhilarating mineral; it can make people talkative and eloquent. Because of this, it reduces inhibitions and, in the form of mica water, it makes a good remedy for timidity, stage fright, and cowardice.

Zodiac Correspondences

Mica will calm Pisces and coax Cancer out of its shell.

MOLDAVITE

Chemical composition: Silicon and aluminum oxide

Color: Translucent, olive to bottle green

Principal deposits: Moldavia; similar stones have been found in Australia and the United States (Georgia)

Hardness: 5.5

Density: 3.9 to 4

Etymology and General Characteristics

Moldavite owes its name to a body of water, the Moldau, which was immortalized by the composer Smetana. There is only one deposit of moldavite in the world. Australite and georgiaite look similar but don't equal it in brilliance. Some of these rocks were found molten under the impact of meteors.

Moldavite is useful for personal development. It is said to enhance intuition and telepathic gifts.

Therapeutic Uses

A rejuvenating stone, moldavite stimulates personal fulfillment and slows down the aging process. Like many green stones, it is excellent for the eyes. Drinking moldavite water also soothes gas and cardiac weakness. Moldavite simulates memory and protects against mental degeneration. It is an excellent stimulant for treating gout.

Zodiac Correspondences

A green stone, moldavite will help Taurus to see the world clearly. Cancer will become more of a go-getter by wearing a moldavite stone. And Moldavite will bring Capricorn more inner peace.

MOONSTONE

Chemical composition: Feldspar, aluminum, and potassium silicate

Color: A colorless or milky white stone, sometimes showing orangish yellow or blue reflections

Principal deposits: India, Sri Lanka, Madagascar, Brazil, Australia, the Americas, and the Arabian Peninsula

Hardness: 6.5

Density: 2.6

Etymology and General Characteristics

The moonstone evokes the moon, with its milky whiteness and benevolence. Its correspondence with the moon is found in many languages. Cutting this stone gives it a slightly metallic shine.

In India, it was the stone of the gods and goddesses, of hope and spiritual purity through denial of the ego. It combats materialism and strengthens the faith of religious people in all cultures. It has an affinity with hermits, monks, and other contemplatives who have withdrawn from the world.

Moonstone is also the stone of love and eroticism; it activates our carnal desires. It can also transcend them and help us to experience a mystical love. It is a feminine, even "female" stone. Women will relate to this stone and find that some of their emotional blockages vanish as if in a dream. The moonstone has an animal sensuality and will help men to get in touch with their feminine side.

But the moonstone's apparent calm can also give way to tumultuous inner storms, which can end up "exploding" and spilling out onto others. It is the stone of contained passions that have suddenly become torrid.

It is also the stone of the "love-seer." It helps people know the destiny of their beloved, to warn him or her of any future danger. In addition, it protects travelers.

Therapeutic Uses

A stone of fertility, it is used in Arabia, Yemen, the Maghreb (North Africa), and Sicily by women who want to have a baby. To use the stone in this way, sew it into the hem of a garment. Moonstone also regularizes the female cycle. And placed between the breasts, it noticeably increases lactation.

The moonstone, as the stone of carnal communion, has an aphrodisiac effect. In general its effects are delayed and may take several days to appear. For those suffering from impotence, frigidity, or low libido, it is best to avoid holding it for too long since once the stone begins working, the powerful effects can be embarrassing.

Moonstone assures the drainage of the lymphatic system. It is a growth stone for children and teenagers, and it slows the degeneration of old people. It also enhances beneficial dreams and helps us to easily understand them.

Zodiac Correspondences

This lunar stone has a special affinity with the maternal sign of Cancer. Cancer's eroticism will be strengthened—under the covers, imagination will be king!

Those born under the sign of Capricorn will find it easier to express their emotions when wearing the moonstone. Pisces' ability to concentrate will be helped by looking at this stone for one minute, three times a day.

NEPHRITE

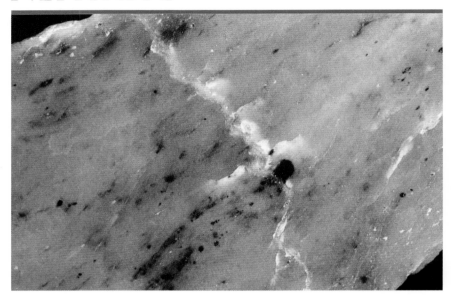

Chemical composition: Basic magnesium calcium iron silicate

Color: Green, tending toward gray, with white marbling

Principal deposits: China, Japan, Tibet, Mexico, and Peru

Hardness: 6 to 6.5

Density: 3.2

Etymology and General Characteristics

A near homonym of nephritis, a painful kidney ailment (coming from *nephros,* "kidney" in Greek), nephrite owes its name to its ability to cure kidney disease. This stone looks like jade. Very beautiful objects are cut from nephrite, but it is best known for its therapeutic qualities.

Therapeutic Uses

This stone treats kidney disease. If kidney problems persist and are inherited or psychosomatic, combine this stone with tourmaline. Nephrite water energizes the kidney function.

This is also an excellent stone for aging animals; it will help old cats and dogs who are incontinent. Nephrite is used for the big cats in menageries and zoos when they are sick and old. The animal should wear a nephrite stone on its collar.

Zodiac Correspondences

Nephrite, a stone that is mainly therapeutic is not connected to any sign in particular. It can heal kidney problems in all of the signs. However, it acts faster on Pisces and Cancer.

OBSIDIAN

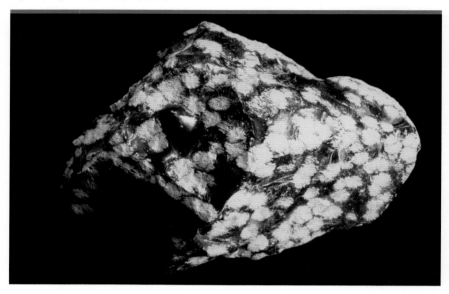

Chemical composition: Siliceous volcanic stone

Color: Black, dark brown, black and silver, or black and gold

Principal deposits: Iceland, Greece, Italy (Sicily), Mexico; more generally, volcanic lands and the major faults in the earth's layer, the limits of the tectonic plates

Hardness: 5 to 5.5

Density: 2.5 to 2.7

Etymology and General Characteristics

From the Greco-Latin *obsidios* that, according to the ancient philosopher Pliny the Elder's *Natural Histories,* was named after Obsius, a Hellenized Roman who discovered this stone.

North American Indians used obsidian a great deal to make cult objects, arrow tips, and javelins, as well as daggers for human sacrifices. In Mexico, obsidian is thought to be the son of the primordial couple that founded all of creation. For the ancient Mexicans, the "obsidian

years" corresponded to lean years dominated by aridity, drought, and infertility.

The obsidian's radiance makes it a sacred, magical stone. Despite the beauty and the fascination that cut obsidian holds, we mustn't forget that it is a flint (a stone made up of silica). This fire stone can produce sparks when shaken up; it can even set a household on fire.

Obsidian, actually a cold stone, comes from the most extreme heat, the heart of volcanoes, from the magma. It balances opposites. It makes us more familiar with the mysteries of our hidden lives and will lead us to "remove the mask," and discover who we really are inside. This brings with it many surprises, some of them revealing the exact opposite of what we've believed!

Therapeutic Uses

The Aztecs made a balm for healing scars that contained obsidian powder. In fact, they believed that the same substance that made weapons could also heal the wounds they created. This practice was also found in the north of France and in Belgium, though there was no contact between the Aztecs and these two countries. The flint powder or obsidian was mixed with rabbit and chamomile grease, according to various secret recipes that female sorcerers and local healers guarded jealously.

Looking at a black obsidian for half an hour each day for seven days will help us to know ourselves better. The mental "mirror effect" will put us in touch with our deeper selves. It activates the will, especially in cases of depression, but it will not heal the depression itself. You can add a rock crystal to it for that effect.

Zodiac Correspondences

This stone has an affinity with Scorpio, Taurus, and Gemini, the signs said to have two sides. This is an antischizophrenic stone that could have cured Doctor Jekyll!

Obsidian will help those born under the signs of Capricorn and Sagittarius to get in touch with their deepest feelings and needs.

OLIVINE

Chemical composition: Magnesium and iron silicate

Color: This stone is an olive green chrysolite.

Principal deposits: Red Sea, Myanmar (Burma), South Africa, Australia, United States, Brazil, and Congo (Zaire)

Hardness: 6.5

Density: 3.30

Etymology and General Characteristics

The name of this stone comes from its color. This stone stimulates an inner opening, the desire to serve the world in some way—to offer oneself to a cause, to love, to life. It is the stone of those who make a vow, or who are ready to take on a deep passion.

Therapeutic Uses

Olivine works against emotional coldness and it stimulates enthusiasm. It also strengthens the myocardium. It is the stone of poetic inspiration and eloquence. It protects fiery temperaments against fits of temper.

An olivine stone should always be worn alone.

Zodiac Correspondences

Pisces will be protected against harmful influences—cheating, slander, or attempted swindling. It will also help heal cardiovascular problems for Pisces and Leo. Olivine will inspire Leos to express themselves with eloquence and passion.

ONYX

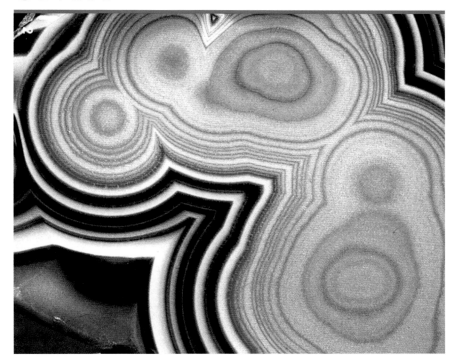

Chemical composition: Silicon dioxide

Color: This stone is a black agate beribboned in white. The onyx veined in white and dark brown or red is called sardonyx.

Principal deposits: Those of agate—South America, India, and Germany

Hardness: 6 to 6.5

Density: 2 to 2.5

Etymology and General Characteristics

From the Greek *onux,* meaning "fingernail." Legend has it that Cupid was in the midst of cutting Venus's nails one day as she was sleeping, and the clippings fell onto the ground. The Fates immediately transformed them into stone believing that nothing that comes from a goddess should perish.

This stone is connected to the body, to belonging to the earth or clan, to putting down roots. It can also represent family discord. It was reputed to separate lovers.

In China, only slaves extracted it; a free man would not have exposed himself to the danger of this "bad-luck stone." It was reputed to be fatal for pregnant women and was believed to bring on nightmares.

However, the Persians in antiquity had the opposite belief. They believed that on the contrary, onyx helped during childbirth and protected people from the evil eye.

A stone representing both sides of the coin—connection and discord, the onyx is both claw and fingernail; it will attack evil and good with the same violence. Moreover, it encourages abrupt changes in mood, even depression. This doesn't prevent onyx from being widely used in rings and other jewelry.

It is the stone of plots and machinations. The aggressiveness produced by this stone is favorable for businesspeople and conquerors. Sardonyx—the variety veined in white and dark brown or red—will correct this stone's aggressive aspect by encouraging friendship, or rather complicity, an often temporary alliance against a common enemy or a "whipping boy."

Therapeutic Uses

Protects against accidents. Helps in concentration. It is the supreme remedy for buzzing in the ears and deafness.

However, it is advisable not to wear this stone continuously. Holding it in your hand for 10 minutes several times during the day is an excellent practice, particularly before a negotiation, a request for a salary increase, or a raise. Beware of possible side effects: aggressiveness, gloominess, and depression.

Zodiac Correspondences

Onyx is Scorpio's favorite stone. It will stabilize the volatile emotions of those born under this sign.

This stone will help Capricorn, too much of an individualist at times, to be more of a team player.

OPAL

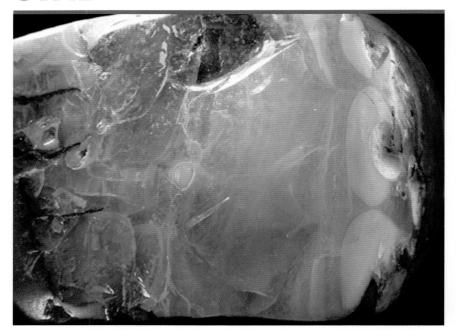

Chemical composition: Quartz with miniscule watery incrustations

Color: Opals have a colorless, whitish hue, with sparkling iridescence due to the water they contain. Opals can also be yellow, blue, black, or green. There are also ruby-red, orange opals called "fire opals."

Principal deposits: Australia, the Czech Republic, Brazil, and Mexico

Hardness: 5 to 6.5

Density: 2 to 2.3

Etymology and General Characteristics

From the Latin word *opalus,* with the same meaning. The word may relate to the goddess Ops, an earthly power and Saturn's spouse, who was later comparable with Cybele.

It's the stone of white light, of that merciless brightness of the northern countrysides. The seven colors of the rainbow play hide-and-seek in this stone; the opalescences often seem to disappear as soon as you try to focus on them.

Something fleeting emanates from this stone that often seems to cover its disquieting aspects. This stone was once suspected of bringing bad luck. The Empress Eugénie was afraid of it after having an accident in a carriage called the Opal.

At the same time, it was considered to be a talisman that would allow a person to recognize his enemies—and friends. When in the presence of an enemy, the opal would grow pale; with friends, it would turn red with pleasure.

An ancient legend had it that opal could make a person invisible under certain conditions. In Rome, it was nicknamed *patronus furum,* "the boss of thieves" who, once they were invisible, could get into rich people's homes easily.

Yet it is also a beneficent, lunar stone—peaceful, prosperous, and changeable. It asks that we become attached to it, to "understand" it. As soon as this happens, it will serve us faithfully.

Therapeutic Uses

Opal's calming, even sedative effect doesn't stop it from stimulating the myocardium.

All opals help to create a sense of calm and reduce depression. Dark or black opals drive away "wild imaginings," subliminal, nocturnal deliriums rather than true nightmares. This stone helps us to stop brooding so we can better direct our thoughts. A stone of clarity, opal fortifies memory and strengthens the visual faculties.

The fire opal can cure all digestive problems.

Zodiac Correspondences

Another lunar stone, the opal has a strong affinity with the maternal sign of Cancer. This stone will encourage Cancers to think carefully before acting. It will also help Pisces make solid, secure decisions.

Headstrong Aries will discover that calm strength is often more effective than aggressive behavior. The opal's antidepressive effects will be especially useful for those born under the signs of Sagittarius and Aquarius and can boost their confidence.

ORPIMENT

Chemical composition: Arsenic and sulfur

Color: Golden or lemon yellow; orpiment can be transparent or translucent.

Principal deposits: Russia, Turkey, Asia Minor, Hungary, and France

Hardness: 1.5 to 2

Density: 3.4 to 3.5

Etymology and General Characteristics

From the Latin *aurum pigmentum,* meaning "gold painting." In ancient times, people believed that this soft stone actually contained gold. Legend has it that icon painters used it for their paintings of Christ and the saints. Because their works were often destroyed by heretics, they worked in secret. Not wanting to be caught acquiring gold, which was needed for sacred Greco-Byzantine paintings, they gathered orpiment, ground it up, and used it as a substitute. Orpiment is brilliant yellow rather gold in color, and it is still used today in many kinds of paintings.

Therapeutic Uses

The powerful, yellow color of orpiment makes it a kind of electrical battery or "booster," which strengthens the action of the complementary stones—which are purple, mauve, blue, or red in color. It is the supreme remedy for sadness, gloominess, and depression. Orpiment represents self-confidence and the joy of living. It has a significant aphrodisiac effect, and it restores one's appetite while preventing digestive problems. It is also a good remedy for insomnia as long as you never use it at night or after four o'clock in the afternoon.

Orpiment is also one of the main sources of pharmaceutical arsenic.

Zodiac Correspondences

This stone will have an invigorating effect on all the signs. It will especially stimulate Virgos, and give them the daring they often lack. Leos will find a complementary sense of dignity in this golden stone that will chase away their occasional fits of sadness. Taurus and Libra will also bathe in this solar light. This brilliant stone will boost their self-confidence, and fill them with the joy of living.

PEARL

Chemical composition: Calcium carbonate

Color: White and, more rarely, black

Principal deposits: Persian Gulf, Indian Ocean, Japan, Australia, and Isthmus of Panama

Hardness: 2.5 to 4

Density: 2.6 to 2.9

Etymology and General Characteristics

From the Latin word *perla,* with the same meaning. Pearls are made up of concentric layers of mother-of-pearl (aragonite) placed around a core that can be a minuscule grain of sand. They are the result of the oyster's organic self-defense mechanism. The mollusk's secretions incorporate all foreign bodies so as to make them inoffensive to its organism.

This defense does not destroy the potential enemy. On the contrary, it envelops and incorporates it. The pearl is called the "Divine Mother" in India. It represents a symbolic gestation beginning with the element that it covers up. It protects what could have been dangerous.

This symbolizes how the twists and turns of life can cause us to rebound—and be reborn. Each experience perfects us and brings us back to the world. The mother-of-pearl "shell" does not isolate us; on the contrary, it vibrates in unison with the world and helps us to look at life more deeply. It is also a lesson in tolerance; instead of chasing away the intruder, the oyster welcomes it, integrates it, and makes it a creative experience—which generates rebirth and new beginnings.

This aura of rebirth explains why in ancient Greece, the pearl was considered a way to combat the aging process. It was said that Cleopatra applied it topically, dissolved in vinegar, to stay young and beautiful.

Pearls were said to cure madness in ancient Rome. They also cured gastric problems in China. Sailors and pirates of the eighteenth century put a pearl into lemon juice or warm orange juice. They often added rum or schiedam (juniper alcohol or gin) to it. This beverage protected them from scurvy (due actually to the vitamin C contained in the lemon or orange).

When a pearl turns dull, it is said to "die." But pay attention—this is often the sign of a challenge or illness for its owner. More rarely, this disquieting sign may concern the person who gave the pearl as a gift. Cultured pearls have the same effects as natural pearls.

Therapeutic Uses

Pearls are made up of calcium. They become activated when in contact with the skin and they strengthen the effect of medicinal calcium or that contained in mineral water. In cases of decalcification, it is beneficial to roll a pearl along the afflicted bones.

A "dead" pearl can be dissolved in vinegar. The pearly vinegar can then be used to rub lightly on your temples if you have gloomy ideas, depression, suicidal tendencies, or an obsession with death.

Instead of a remedy for a specific infection, this stone should be used as a catalyst to strengthen the effects of other gems. In addition, the pearl stabilizes and intensifies our inner radiance.

Zodiac Correspondences

Water signs will feel in harmony with the pearl. It will help Cancer and Pisces, in particular, to weather the ups and downs of life. It will remind those born under these signs of their inner richness.

The rare black pearl is another stone that will give Virgo the daring it often lacks.

The pearl will also help those born under the sign of Capricorn in relationships—whether in love or business.

PERIDOT

Chemical composition: A variety of Chrysolite

Color: Lime, olive, yellowish green, or medium dark green hues

Principal deposits: Red Sea, Australia, South Africa, Brazil, United States (Hawaii, Arizona), Congo (Zaire), and Norway

Hardness: 6.5 to 7

Density: 3.2 to 3.3

Etymology and General Characteristics

A strange stone with an uncertain name! It may stem from the Arab *faridat,* meaning "precious stone."

Peridot was brought back to Europe from the Orient by the crusaders. Italian and Flemish artisans used it to make cult objects. Peridots of "extraterrestrial" origin were found in a meteorite that fell in 1749 in Eastern Silesia, Poland.

This stone enhances emotional clarity; it transforms instinct into feeling, desire into tenderness, attraction into calm love, and passion into long-lasting tenderness. Gold is the metal that enhances peridot, both aesthetically and therapeutically.

Therapeutic Uses

The peridot purifies the body and fights chronic constipation. It is a very good hepatic and renal regulator. This stone also enhances clear-sightedness.

Peridot decreases anxiety, impatience, and stage fright. This stone also chases away depressing ideas, encourages forgiveness, and strengthens common sense.

Zodiac Correspondences

The strong and aggressive signs of Scorpio, Leo, and Aries will be helped by this stone. Peridot will curb their impatience and make them more tolerant of others. It will also help the Aries natives to turn their impulsive attractions into lasting love.

PYRITE

Chemical composition: Iron sesquioxide

Color: Pale, dull gold or yellowish gray

Principal deposits: Pyrite is found throughout the world—especially the Amazon and France (Elba Island, near Corsica).

Hardness: 6 to 6.5

Density: 5

Etymology and General Characteristics

From the Greek *pyros,* meaning "fire." When pyrite is struck against a metal, stone, or hard surface, it will emit sparks.

It is also called "fool's gold" and in Germany, "cats' gold." The Incas made mirrors out of it. Its sparkle and brilliance evoke real gold. This is why dishonest mine owners used to salt their mines with pyrite, to make people believe they were still gold-producers. Naive gold prospectors sometimes confused pyrite and gold, which explains the name "fool's gold."

It is the talisman stone of the fire trades: bakers, blacksmiths, and firemen. It also protects people in the building trades.

Therapeutic Uses

As a pendant, pyrite enhances the action of the respiratory tract. Don't be alarmed at the small traces it can leave on the skin; it's easy to wash off. Pyrite's action often gets fast results. For cases in which no resolution looks possible, as well as in instances of intellectual fatigue from overworking and tiredness of the nervous system, pyrite will be beneficial. It "restructures" the cognitive faculties and strengthens our organizational abilities. Last of all, it stimulates memory.

Zodiac Correspondences

The qualities of pyrite have an affinity with Gemini's intellect. This stone will help those born under this sign to be more focused—centering their numerous, and often disparate, interests.

Pyrite's shiny quality will attract the royal lion. This stone will enhance Leo's creativity and make him a bit less demanding and haughty. His concentration will also be improved.

RHODOCHROSITE

Chemical composition: Manganese carbonate; it sometimes contains calcium or ferrous iron instead of manganese.

Color: White or pinkish red, in alternately light and dark streaks; transparent or opaque

Principal deposits: Argentina, United States (Colorado), and Central and South America

Hardness: 4

Density: 3.3 to 3.7

Etymology and General Characteristics

From the Greek *rhodon,* which means "rose," this rose-colored stone encourages meditation. It enables us to go within and find effective solutions to our problems. Rhodochrosite can help us become mature adults and heal the wounds of childhood. It can help us to better

understand and forgive our parents. This stone also helps those who work with children—pediatricians, elementary school teachers, and caregivers.

Therapeutic Uses

Rhodochrosite directly attacks somatizations, the physical disorders that stem from emotional or mental suffering. It is especially effective with skin disorders. Shingles, a painful viral infection caused by the chicken pox virus, can appear when we are depressed or in mourning. Rhodochrosite can easily control this condition. The same is true for some types of hives and boils.

This stone can have a spectacular effect on Parkinson's disease. However, it can't cure it; this stone is only an aid in relieving symptoms of this serious illness. (See Rhodonite for specific treatment instructions.) The same is true for some cases of multiple sclerosis. Impotence can also be treated with rhodochrosite.

Zodiac Correspondences

This pink stone is suitable for Cancer natives. It will help them to love themselves so they can more easily love others.

Rhodochrosite will balance the emotional ups and downs of those born under the sign of Taurus.

RHODONITE

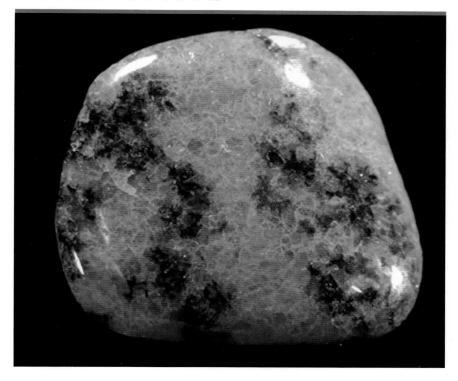

Chemical composition: Manganese metasilicate

Color: Rose with black streaks; can be opaque or transparent. The yellowish brown variety is called fowlerite.

Principal deposits: India, Mexico, Madagascar, Sweden, and Russia (Ural Mountains)

Hardness: 5.5 to 6.5

Density: 3.4 to 3.7

Etymology and General Characteristics

Rhodochrosite's "sister" stone, rhodonite has a more intense color. Its effects are approximately the same, but the action of this stone is slower, deeper, and more lasting. Rhodonite is a calming stone that diminishes stress. It protects us against envy and jealousy by creating an engaging "aura." It is especially effective in reducing the childhood jealousies between siblings that often spoil their adult relationships. Using rhodonite makes it possible to avoid numerous arguments over shared assets, such as an inheritance.

Therapeutic Uses

Treatment can begin by attacking a disturbed area with rhodochrosite, and then continuing a more in-depth treatment with rhodonite.

Parkinson's disease will be relieved by rhodonite, as long as one also closely follows the standard medical treatment. To begin, drink one 8-ounce glass of rhodochrosite water every day for two weeks. Follow that with rhodonite water every day for three weeks. Next, massage your hands with a polished rhodonite stone for a good 15 minutes a day for one week. The trembling will be diminished.

This stone can also relieve trembling after heavy drinking. But in no way can it cure alcoholism; this requires a treatment that includes counseling as well as medication in some cases.

Obsessive jealousies can be soothed by rhodonite, as can mild forms of paranoia.

Zodiac Correspondences

Those of rhodochrosite, with the addition of Leos, who are often too sure of themselves. Rhodonite also fights against their tendency to be snobbish.

ROSE QUARTZ

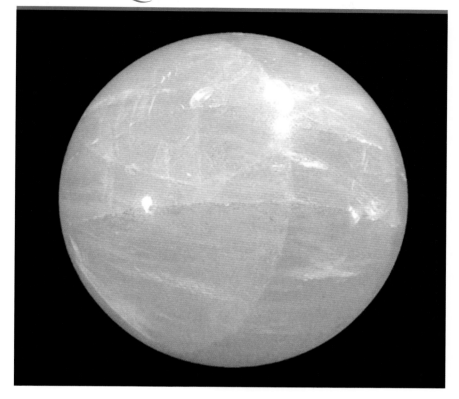

Chemical composition: Silicon dioxide

Color: Pale pink to rosy red

Principal deposits: Austria, Uganda, Madagascar, Brazil, Russia (Ural Mountains), and North America

Hardness: 7

Density: 2.6

Etymology and General Characteristics

See smoky quartz for etymology and more general qualities of quartz. Rose quartz is sometimes called hyaline quartz, from the Greek *hyalos*, meaning "glass." This is a stone of love, tenderness, and sensuality. This stone's soft rose color gives off a gentle vibration that contrasts with the hardiness of the mines and the men who work in them.

Australian sorcerers make a powerful, sacred water out of this stone that they call liquefied quartz; they consider this liquid to be a panacea. A powerful aura of magic emanates from quartz, especially from rose quartz with its sometimes carnal reflections.

Therapeutic Uses

An effective detoxification agent, rose quartz was long considered a universal antidote to poison. But it actually heals physical problems connected to emotional wounds. A rose quartz necklace will soothe cardiac problems due to the pain of lost love. A powerful aphrodisiac, this stone also stimulates the sensual imagination.

Rose quartz reduces blisters if you rub them lightly with a polished stone. You can also diminish the appearance of unsightly scars.

Zodiac Correspondences

The quartzes are universal stones that relate to all the signs. They represent human destiny in general. However, rose quartz will strengthen the romantic ardor of those born under the sign of Taurus. This stone will also strengthen Libra's determination.

RUBY

Chemical composition: Aluminum oxide

Color: This stone is a variety of red corundum. It can also be pink, or a shade going toward blue. Some stones are a deeper wine-color.

Principal deposits: Southeast Asia, Tanzania, Norway, and Sri Lanka

Hardness: 9

Density: 3.9 to 4

Etymology and General Characteristics

From *rubeus,* or "red" in Latin. The queen of stones and the stone of kings, rubies are majestic. They often ornament scepters, crowns, and other symbols of power. The ruby symbolizes the strength of love, but domination as well; with this stone, balance is hard to achieve.

The ruby is an aphrodisiac and will enable you to experience all forms of love, from wild sensuality to mystical communion. It completes and deepens a couple's relationship and encourages closeness without merging—if we know how to resist the will for power and domination. Combining ruby with a moonstone or rock crystal can help maintain balance. Even so, watch out for jealousy.

Rubies are also the stone of courtly love and inspire passion at a distance. Sucking on a ruby will allow you to make eloquent declarations of love. However, if the love dies, the ruby's action will be inflexible, even cruel; it is the hardest stone after the diamond.

Rubies are concentrated fire, burning embers. They are the emblem of flamboyant happiness. But watch out; if a ruby changes color, it can foretell misfortune. It is important to know yourself quite well before wearing a ruby. Prudence is necessary; this stone can spill everything it possesses that is dark and disturbing over your soul, in contrast with the stone's beautiful, limpid, red color.

Therapeutic Uses

A blood stone, rubies strengthen the myocardium and the coronaries; they were used for a long time to prevent hemorrhaging. Rubies alleviate menstrual pain and help make menstruation regular. It is the ideal remedy for sexual problems, and for misunderstandings between partners. It was once thought to protect against venereal diseases. In the Middle Ages it was the protective stone of the prostitutes of Les Halles in Paris.

Rubies correct the effects of depression without healing it in depth. It should only be used for this purpose as a supplement to another, more standard treatment. This stone also aids memory.

Zodiac Correspondences

The ruby is tailor-made for the royal sign of Leo. Aries, another fire sign, also has an affinity with this stone. The red can exacerbate the natural aggressiveness of those born under these signs. It's important to not wear the red stone constantly if you have a tendency to lose your temper. Wearing a ruby (with the same precautions) can also help Scorpio correct his negativity.

SAPPHIRE

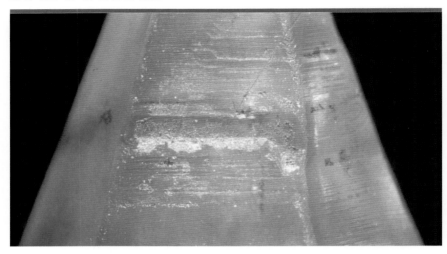

Chemical composition: Aluminum oxide

Color: This stone is a blue variety of the corundum. Sapphires can be found in all shades of blue, but occasionally also yellow, orange, green, purple, and, more rarely, black.

Principal deposits: Southeast Asia, Sri Lanka, and Australia

Hardness: 9

Density: 4

Etymology and General Characteristics

From the Latin *sapphirus,* derived from the Greek *sappheiros,* meaning "blue stone." The Greek word came from a Semitic language that took it from the Sanskrit *sanipryâm.* Sapphires bring love of justice, the thirst for truth. According to Louis XI's lapidary (an expert in precious stones), "meditating on this stone brings the soul to contemplate the heavens." We know that this king meditated long and hard and had great religious feeling—which didn't prevent him from being cruel. Moreover, he had the reputation of holding onto anger, as powerful people can do.

This is the stone of attachment. Like rubies, sapphires are almost as

hard as diamonds. It is advisable to remove a sapphire ring when undergoing a separation or divorce. Sapphires are thought to prolong an attachment, and they could become malevolent. If the stone was given as a gift by the person from whom you are separating, it would be best to give it back.

Therapeutic Uses

Sapphires free us from our "inner prisons" and the psychic suffering that can cause us to shut down emotionally. It can be used as an aid to treatments for neuroses or even psychosis. This stone is also a good remedy for eye problems. Sapphire water, used for ablutions or drinking, is a good purifier that should be taken when the seasons change. Wearing a sapphire on the heart area will relieve allergies, particularly asthma. Sapphires soothe insomnia. A stone placed on the forehead reduces fever and stops nosebleeds.

Zodiac Correspondences

Blue sapphire will encourage Taurus natives to look within and discover the subtle forces that affect their lives. Yellow sapphire will make it easier for shy Virgos to express themselves verbally.

The sapphire will stimulate a spiritual search for those born under the sign of Libra. It will also stimulate new ideas, and creative "leaps" for the future-oriented sign of Aquarius. Sagittarians should meditate on this stone when they need to make an important, life-changing decision.

SILICIFIED WOOD

Chemical composition: This substance is formed by the silicification of wood. Because each piece of wood is silicified in its own particular geochemical environment, the materials each piece contains will vary greatly. The silica usually forms chalcedony, jasper, or opal. The dead wood disappears and is gradually replaced with the stone.

Color: Silicified wood has sparkling designs and lined veins. It is brown, reddish brown, or light brown.

Principal deposits: Silicified wood is found just about everywhere in the world, especially in Egypt, Argentina, and Nevada. The most spectacular deposit is the "petrified forest" in Holbrook, Arizona, which dates back two hundred million years and includes araucaria trunks having a diameter of twenty-one feet.

Hardness: That of the stone from which it is formed

Density: That of the stone from which it is formed

Etymology and General Characteristics

Silicified wood brings together the symbolism of the mineral and vegetable worlds. The memory of vegetation connects it to the nutrition of the earth. Silicified wood represents time that has stopped or life in suspension—the moment that flows slowly before a catastrophe. This stone marks a new stage of existence; the survival after the Apocalypse. It is also a talismanic stone that sailors carried to guard against shipwreck.

Therapeutic Uses

Silicified wood is beneficial for all types of convalescence. It also has the same therapeutic qualities as chalcedony, jasper, and opal. This stone is helpful in pregnancy and everything that requires maturation. In certain regions it was used to slow down the ripening of wine, so it would not become bitter. These stones increase appetite and are suitable for the treatment of anorexics.

Zodiac Correspondences

Silicified wood is beneficial for Libra, Virgo, and Taurus natives. See also the zodiac correspondences for chalcedony, jasper, and opal.

SMOKY QUARTZ

Chemical composition: Silicon dioxide

Color: This stone is found in various shades of black and brown.

Principal deposits: Austria, Uganda, Madagascar, Brazil, Russia (Ural Mountains), and North America

Hardness: 7

Density: 2.6

Etymology and General Characteristics

Smoky quartz is a variety of rock crystal. It has the latter's qualities but its effects are less radical. The name relates to *quadertz,* an old German word for a bad mineral. This stone is sometimes mistakenly called "smoky topaz." The darkest varieties of smoky quartz are called "morion," from the old French *moreau,* meaning "black."

The quartz stones symbolize resurrection and rebirth. They personify the dark forces, the underlying life, the hidden fire. Quartz possesses an invigorating power. It represents determination, the survival instinct, the fight against annihilation. It also relates to germination, the slow birth from the seed buried in the ground or the maturation of insects such as the beetle that start their growth in the ground before flying away.

Therapeutic Uses

Smoky quartz protects the pulmonary tracts and regenerates the bronchi. This stone can also help you to quit smoking. Suck on a piece of it before each cigarette, or even while smoking. Little by little, the desire to smoke will fade away. Quartz—whether it is smoky or rose—can stimulate the will to live. Smoky quartz is also an aphrodisiac and can enhance unions that are both carnal and mystical. It carries within it the sometimes rough sensuality of the earth's entrails.

Zodiac Correspondences

Smoky quartz has an affinity with all the signs. It can reduce the Capricorn native's tendency toward self-criticism and give gentle Libra the courage to look within and heal long buried wounds.

SODALITE

Chemical composition: Aluminum sodium silicate and feldspar

Color: Cutting makes this dull, blue, opaque stone shiny.

Principal deposits: Africa, Brazil, Canada, and India

Hardness: 5 to 6

Density: 2.2 to 2.4

Etymology and General Characteristics

From the Latin *sodium*, or soda. Sodalite is a calming stone that encourages spirituality and deep thinking. It strengthens concentration and aids meditation. It helps us to both look within and to remain true to ourselves. It also corrects excessive aggressiveness and mockery.

Lapis lazuli is usually used in place of sodalite because its effects are more powerful.

Therapeutic Uses

Sodalite encourages relaxation and fights guilty feelings and irrational fears. It does not otherwise have a specific therapeutic effect. It contributes to our general well-being and combines very well with other stones used to treat a particular illness.

Zodiac Correspondences

Sodalite will help to reduce the conformist tendencies of those born under the sign of Virgo. It will also help Sagittarians to be less dependent on the opinions of others.

SULFUR

Chemical composition: Sulfur

Color: A translucent and fragile yellow stone with a sometimes adamantine brilliance.

Principal deposits: A very widespread substance

Hardness: 1.5

Density: 2.05 to 2.08

Etymology and General Characteristics

From the Latin *sulphur,* with the same meaning. This mineral, connected to fire, burns easily. In the Bible, it is a symbol of sterility.

Sulfur is the active principle of alchemists, one that can "kill" or "fertilize" bright silver (mercury). It is, for the body, what the sun is for the universe. It can fortify and restore our failing faculties. However, sulfur evokes the hell promised to vain selfishness that does not seek wisdom for itself and that becomes its own divinity. A rain of sulfur was Sodom's punishment.

In some esoteric traditions, sulfur is thought to be the "mineral sperm," the breath of fire that gives life. Sulfur's clarity while burning is considered an "antilight," a clarity fatal to Lucifer's pride. Sulfur therefore drives away bad influences, protects against the evil eye, and disenchants.

Therapeutic Uses

Sulfur fights fever and inflammations and cures colds. It should be taken in small doses (a pinch in a glass of distilled water).

Zodiac Correspondences

Sulfur will have a balancing effect on Virgo and Cancer natives.

SUNSTONE

Chemical composition: Sodium and calcium aluminosilicate

Color: An orange, dark brown, colorless, or red stone

Principal deposits: Canada, United States, Norway, India, and Russia (Ural Mountains)

Hardness: 6 to 6.5

Density: 2.6

Etymology and General Characteristics

The sunstone is also called oligoclase. It contains hematite or goethite particles. This feldspar is connected to carnelian through its medicinal applications. It does, however, add a certain vital force. The sunstone twinkles and fascinates through its shininess in motion. But be careful: this stone is very fragile.

The sunstone relates to people of faith—missionaries and others who give themselves in service to the world. It helps us to act with grace and aids in active, joyous meditation.

Therapeutic Uses

The sunstone is used to treat cramps, fevers, and various infections. It also treats osteoarthritis, arthritis, and vision and kidney problems. It is an antidepressant that acts gradually on a short-term basis. It chases away nightmares.

It has a progressive aphrodisiac effect. It can provide relief, which will last about a week, for temporary impotence or frigidity. Massage the concerned organs with this stone.

Zodiac Correspondences

Sunstone will bring out the sensuality of those born under the sign of Virgo. This stone will temper the sexuality and possessiveness of the Aries native.

TANZANITE

Chemical composition: Calcium and aluminum silicate

Color: A variety of zoisite, this stone is deep purple-blue in color

Principal deposits: Tanzania (eastern Africa)

Hardness: 6.5 to 7

Density: 3.3

Etymology and General Characteristics

Tanzanite was discovered in 1954 in Arusha, Tanzania, and made fashionable by the jeweler Tiffany who created magnificent jewels to showcase this stone.

Therapeutic Uses

This recently discovered stone has not revealed all its secrets. Like other varieties of zoisite, tanzanite works well combined with other stones.

It is excellent for the problem of excessive sweating. It is also used for psychological disorders, stress, and nervous tension. Tanzanite should be placed for 5 minutes daily on the areas to be treated. Placed on the forehead, it relieves migraine headaches. Tanzanite can also help to cure chronic alcoholism (in conjunction with other treatments such as counseling).

Zodiac Correspondences

Pisces will be soothed by the sparkle of tanzanite. Its iridescence will also please Aries.

TIGER'S EYE

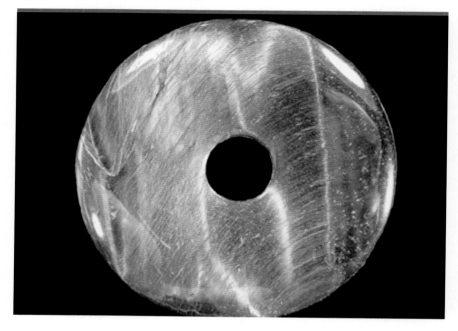

Chemical composition: Quartz in strips connected by layers of asbestos and hornblend

Color: Varieties are based on color and include tiger's eye, falcon's eye, cat's eye, and bull's eye. Tiger's eye, containing more iron and limonite oxide, is golden brown. Falcon's eye is blue-black, cat's eye is green or greenish gray, and bull's eye is a mahogany color.

Principal deposits: The western region of the Australian continent, Myanmar (Burma), South Africa, India, and the Americas

Hardness: 6.5 to 7

Density: 2.5 to 2.7

Etymology and General Characteristics

These stones owe their name to the animals they resemble. The cat's and bull's eye varieties have more or less the same qualities and are

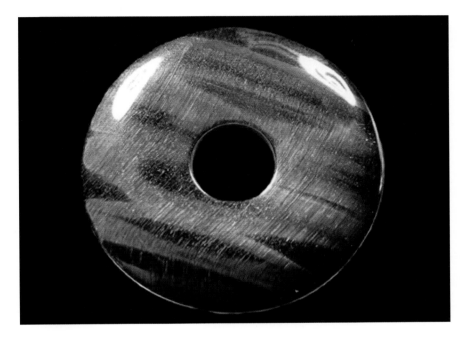

modified by the radiance of their colors. Tiger's eye enhances self-confidence, boldness, and sometimes pride. The falcon's eye can protect us from nightmares. These stones are often confused. For example, some will call tiger's eye the cat's eye and so on.

All varieties of these stones bring good luck and ward off unfavorable energy. They are used a great deal in voodoo rituals. The "eyes" are helpful to our inner vision. These stones can help us to better understand the cause and effect of each situation. They allow us to see the consequences of our actions and to make the right decisions. They are among the best aids for resolving a crisis, and preparing ourselves for positive action.

Therapeutic Uses

These stones combat nightmares, cure angina, and strengthen the heart. When worn before a sports competition, they are very helpful for the muscles. They also fight asthma and accelerate the healing of childhood illnesses (especially cat's eye).

Zodiac Correspondences

These beautiful stones will help Gemini natives to see life more clearly. They will also increase their concentration and focus. Tiger's eye will tone down Leo's tendency to be snobbish. These stones will help those born under the sign of Virgo to express their feelings. In addition, these stones, particularly the falcon's eye, will make Aquarians more level-headed and self-assured.

TOPAZ

Chemical composition: Aluminum fluosilicate

Color: This stone can be colorless, yellow, dark brown, light blue, gold, or pink.

Principal deposits: Brazil, North America, Sri Lanka, South Africa, and Russia (Ural Mountains)

Hardness: 8

Density: 3.5 to 3.6

Etymology and General Characteristics

From the Greek *topaziôn,* designating all types of precious stones. It is also the name of an island in the Red Sea. This stone is connected to the sun, especially golden topaz, the best-known variety. Topaz radiates and heats up in a diffuse manner. The gentle warmth of this stone encourages us and fills us with solid, lasting energy. It wipes away tiredness just like the sun's rays.

Blue topaz extends this solar influence to the entire sky. Strength and energy become inspiration, breath, and momentum. It pushes us to let go of any burdensome, emotional routines.

Therapeutic Uses

The action of topaz stones is more general than specific. Even so, topaz is known to heal nosebleeds and skin eruptions. These stones are also quite effective for cardiac pains. They are used for childhood illnesses such as mumps, scarlet fever, and measles. In addition, topaz stones reduce snoring.

Golden topaz is known to fight depression. Yellow topaz is cosmically linked with the solar plexus. Placing the topaz stone above it will bring an intense feeling of well-being. It is an ideal stone for post-operative convalescence. It also activates blood circulation and stops the problem of cold feet.

Topaz is the "gourmets' stone." It livens sensitivity to taste and stimulates the taste buds. It enables those whose taste has become faded, or who have temporarily lost taste sensation, to recover their gastronomic sharpness. Many wine stewards use it before participating in blind tasting contests. Sucking on a topaz before a meal will allow for better appreciation of food and facilitate digestion at the same time.

Blue topaz relates to the head and cranium. It soothes migraine headaches, tightening of the jaws, occipital pains, and that feeling of a vise squeezing your temples.

Zodiac Correspondences

Yellow or golden topaz is one of Gemini's favorite stones. It helps those born under this sign to communicate their knowledge to others. It also guards against their tendency to try to be a "jack of all trades." Golden topaz also has a balancing effect on Libra.

Blue topaz is beneficial to both Sagittarians and Aquarians.

TOURMALINE

Chemical composition: Iron, aluminum, magnesium borosilicates

Color: According to the proportions of its components, this stone can be green, colorless, pink, red, blue, purple, yellow, brown, black, or multicolored.

Principal deposits: North America, Brazil, southwestern Africa, Sri Lanka, Madagascar; a variety called elbaite is found on the island of Elba.

Hardness: 7 to 7.5

Density: 3 to 3.2

Etymology and General Characteristics

Tourmaline represents rising energy. It offers sagittal radiance, a ray beating down like a surgical laser. This subtle energy "targets" its goal with precision. The collaboration of tourmaline and solar rays is spectacular.

Tourmaline has many colors and each is associated with unique characteristics:

Green tourmaline: Also called verdelite, this variety heals and regenerates. It energizes our minds and strengthens our bodies.

Colorless tourmaline: The effect of the colorless stone is the same as green tourmaline, but it acts more slowly.

Pink/Red tourmaline: Pink and red tourmalines, called rubellites and siberites respectively, traditionally quiet our anxieties. They also help with concentration and reflection. Legend has it that Napoleon, in exile on the island of Elba, used elbaite, a local variety of tourmaline also called ivaite.

Multicolored: The pink, two-color tourmalines surrounded by green, heal the pains of love and protect relationships that are just starting.

Blue tourmaline: Blue tourmaline or indicolte, sometimes called indigolite, helps us to free our minds and think "outside the box."

Brown tourmaline: Also called dravite, this variety repels harmful energies and directs them elsewhere, like a lightning rod. It blocks the harmful aspects of some other dark brown/black stones.

Black tourmaline: Schorl, a mineralogist's name, designates the black variety, which often takes the shape of "love arrows" included in some rock crystals.

Therapeutic Uses

Pointed, short tourmaline sticks can be used to apply pressure to painful places, focusing the stone's beneficial energy on a particular area. It can also be used like a magnifying glass to focus a sunbeam on the area to be treated. This should be stopped right before the heat starts to burn or feel uncomfortable. This action can be compared to the way moxas, the burning, Chinese herbal sticks work. The radiation replaces the live heat of that treatment.

Tourmaline is used specifically for motion sickness. It cures nephritis and gives back shine and gloss to nails and hair. It also helps children to learn how to walk. Tourmaline strengthens the sense of smell. In that respect, it also enhances the perception of the pheromones, which produces a definite aphrodisiac effect. The gastronome can use it combined with topaz. Tourmaline can neutralize the harmful rays of computers and microwave ovens. A tourmaline fragment should be stuck to these machines with adhesive tape.

Green tourmaline regularizes tension. For cardiovascular problems, add a pink tourmaline to the chest area. This combination works wonders. Blue tourmaline heals sore throats. It's important never to use tourmaline, especially the red variety, when you are angry, or if you feel animosity toward someone. Calm down first. The same goes for a cantankerous or spiteful person who won't feel the benefits at all.

Zodiac Correspondences

Red tourmaline will reduce jealousy in those born under the sign of Aries. Libra will benefit from pink tourmaline. The red and black tourmalines will help Scorpio to be less demanding—both of himself and others. The green and black tourmalines will help Capricorns to be more expressive.

TURQUOISE

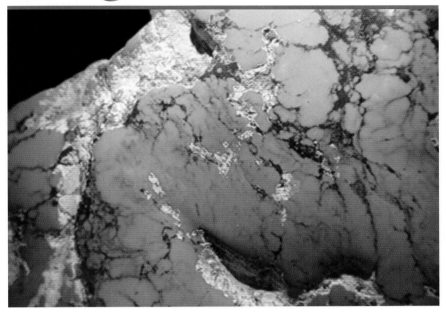

Chemical composition: Basic phosphate hydrated with aluminum and copper

Color: This blue stone has given its name to a very particular color. However, turquoise stones in a stronger blue-green color, or with brown streaks, can also be found.

Principal deposits: Northern Iran, Turkey, China, Australia, United States (Arizona, Nevada), and Israel (Sinai)

Hardness: 5 to 6

Density: 2.6 to 2.8

Etymology and General Characteristics

Turquoise owes its name to Turkey, one of the places where it has long been found. Its waxy look makes it soft to the touch; it's a stone people like to handle and stroke. The sky blue color is mixed with the luxuriant green of nature. This stone represents the balance between heaven and

earth. But it is also the stone of aggression. The incessant wars between the Christian crusaders and the Ottoman world have given scholars a glimpse of how turquoise was used in the Turkish military world.

Warriors wore it as a talisman, and it also ornamented their swords. This stone was said to protect fighters while enhancing their bravery. Turquoise helps to master fear. At the same time, it disposes of compassion. In short, it often "dehumanizes" and this is why it was so useful in war. Real soldiers need to kill methodically, without anger, and warriors—from the knight to the samurai—learned that engaging in combat with a sense of inner calm would ensure victory. Turquoise transforms our own inner negativity—violence, aggressiveness, anger—into positive violence—at least from the military point of view! War's "natural" aspect can be illustrated by the insect world. This may be why wasps and ants imbedded in turquoise were used as amulets in several ancient civilizations.

Pre-Columbian civilizations saw in turquoise the encounter of terrestrial and solar fires—the devastating fire of the cities under siege—and the sun, which was identified with the Great Invincible Warrior.

For the Aztecs, the fire god is called Xiutecuhtli, which means "the turquoise master." The war god, Huitzilopotchli, who is identified with the sun, chases the moon and the stars away each morning, helped by its rays nicknamed "turquoise snakes."

The choice of a turquoise stone as a talisman or gift should not be made lightly. At its best, this stone will help maintain internal balance, and channel aggressiveness into creative projects. At its worst, we may experience a horrible internal war, feelings of self-hatred, self-destruction, and scorn for the human race.

Combining this stone with amber should reduce this danger. Luckily, since it reflects our inner life, the stone itself will warn us of the dangers it can bring on. Turquoise can change color, become dull or even ugly—allowing us to see the state of our mental, spiritual, and physiological health.

Therapeutic Uses

Turquoise, the diagnostic stone, can be "read" by experienced practitioners who can tell which ailment its owner suffers from by examining the changes in its color, the modifications to its touch, and how long it takes to heat up in the hand.

It is better to leave the diagnosing to professionals. We can easily feel alarmed when we see even the slightest modification—a shade that "turns," or tarnishes, for example.

A beautiful, shiny turquoise is helpful to the respiratory system and heals angina. Wearing a turquoise necklace will help to avoid tracheitis and other bronchial attacks. By healing the breath, this stone will cure speech disorders such as stammering. It is also beneficial for the cardiac muscle and the eyes.

In the past, archers and crossbow men were able to strengthen their visual acuity by placing a turquoise stone on their closed eyes. Turquoise gives a certain equanimity of spirit and can drive away nightmares. The strength, balance, and calm this stone can bring is very beneficial for athletes as it can control their emotionalism during competitions.

Zodiac Correspondences

Turquoise will strengthen the will in those born under the sign of Aquarius. It can also heal their liver and pancreatic ailments. Turquoise will strengthen the Pisces natives and calm their often irritating hypersensitivity. This stone will help Sagittarians to negotiate with tact and charm.

ZIRCONIUM

Chemical composition: Zirconium silicate

Color: Colorless to yellowish brown

Principal deposits: Cambodia, Southeast Asia, Sri Lanka, Australia, Brazil, France, and Mozambique

Hardness: 6.5 to 7.5

Density: 3.9 to 4.7

Etymology and General Characteristics

From the Arab *zarkoun,* which means "vermillion," or from the Persian *zargoun,* or "golden." Other etymologies have this word derive from the old French *jargunce,* which became jargon for "small stone."

The fact is that for a long time zirconium cut into gemstones was called "jargon." The origin of the word seems obscure especially since this stone was named in the nineteenth century by the mineralogist A. G. Werner.

Blue zirconium is sometimes called starlite. Zirconium can be slightly radioactive.

Therapeutic Uses

This stone is used for urinary and prostate infections. Zirconium helps people tolerate the effects of the diuretic medication prescribed for some ailments such as cardiac insufficiency and blood problems.

In small amounts, Zirconium's slight radioactivity is not a problem. On the contrary, it stimulates the intellect. You'd have to use several tons of zirconium to have a reaction to its radioactivity.

Zodiac Correspondences

Zirconium reduces depression in Cancerians and nervous tension in Aquarians. It helps to cure the chronic digestive problems of those born under the sign of Sagittarius. They need only to place this stone on the area concerned.

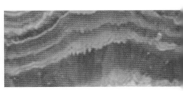

2

APPLYING
THE STONES
THERAPEUTICALLY

This chapter will outline different methods of accessing the therapeutic benefits of the gemstones—from the ancients' use of amulets and talismans to modern forms of jewelry and shaped stones. The form of the stone affects the way in which the healing energy is distributed. Information will also be provided on making the stone waters mentioned elsewhere in the text, applying the stones directly to the body and on the chakras, and contraindications and possible side effects.

AMULETS, CHARMS,
AND TALISMANS

In some of their earliest therapeutic uses, stones were often used in the form of amulets, charms, and other talismans to attract good luck, or to protect against ill fortune. These stones had many functions: some protected the sovereign against assassination, others were used to test food for hidden poisons, and still others were used to attract the benevolence of a particular god. These ancient practices made use of the intrinsic energy of each mineral but also relied on the symbolic powers that were attributed to the artificial or natural shape of a stone.

Raw or Cut and Polished Stones

Some think that raw stones have a more "raw" effect because they are closer to their natural state. This is not always the case. It depends on the stones themselves. Calcite, like chalcedony, "works" perfectly in the raw state. On the other hand, jade and jasper gain additional energy after polishing. In the medieval period, before the invention of faceted cutting, rubies, diamonds, and rock crystals were worn in their raw state or polished and placed in a stud. Modern cutting makes it possible to orient the vibrations and currents of precious stones, which helps to distribute their healing energy more harmoniously.

Sculpted Stones

Sculpted stones have long been used as talismans and amulets. They were sometimes given the shape of the organ to be treated. Chrysolite and turquoise stones cut in the shape of an eye were used to treat eye problems. Heart-shaped agates dating from the late Middle Ages, and amethyst and zirconium amulets in the shape of the male sexual organ have been found. The latter stones were used to treat the venereal diseases that the Roman legionnaires caught from the camp followers of their day. Malachite stones cut in the shape of vulvas were used in Rome and the Far East to cure female illnesses. Jasper and agate were used to sculpt pretty figurines in the form of a pregnant woman to help women bring a pregnancy to term. It is still not known if sculpting increases the force of a stone.

Cameos

Given the beauty and finesse of the cameo engravers' work, it's easy to forget that the actual image held great meaning. The face or profile of the beloved, engraved on a beneficial stone, was meant to bring her luck and protection. The intertwined hands found on the cameos used in engagement rings signified romantic commitment, faith, and fidelity. The dove—as you can guess—was the symbol of peace. The goal was to add a complementary symbolism to the stone's power. Some believed that the stones' beneficial actions were strengthened by these images.

Intaglios

Intalgios, letters or designs engraved on a stone or precious metal, had the same goal. Prayers, incantations, and the words *Allah Akbar* (God is great) were etched on green jade in the lands of Islam. Elsewhere, other stones bear the name of Jupiter or Venus. Still others are engraved with the first words of Ave Maria, or Hebrew characters that begin a particular prayer. Here, the power of faith is combined with the mineral's intrinsic qualities. Judging the effectiveness of these stones is a personal matter that concerns the relation each of us has with the sacred.

MODERN JEWELS

The simplest and most aesthetic way to practice lithotherapy is to wear a stone that corresponds to the problem you want to heal. This can be a raw stone worn on a chain or as an earring, or jewelry ornamented with precious stones cut according to the rules of the art. The particular vibration of each mineral will resonate, first with our skin, and then with our entire beings.

Of course, aesthetics count, and wearing a beautiful jewel can be enjoyable. The mineral influence can also strengthen concentration,

Lapis lazuli necklace

activate meditation, help in emitting alpha waves, or more simply and without your knowing it, help you to have a deep understanding of the text you read, whether it is a newspaper article or a poem. You should be aware that wearing a stone always has an effect. How could you think that matter, charged with vibrations and radiations, could remain inert?

Necklaces and Pendants

A pendant falling onto the chest will radiate like a star on the upper part of the body. Worn close to the throat, it will have an even stronger effect. A jewel worn close to the neck, ornamented with complementary stones corresponding to the owner's health status, will provide an effective element of prevention.

Earrings

Classic or pierced earrings can have a therapeutic effect. You can add aural acupuncture to the effects of lithotherapy as the meridians in the ear correspond to other areas of the body. You can refer to books on aural acupuncture to find a correspondence between the aural area, the stone, and its vibration.

Other Piercings

The navel, nipples, and genital area are significant parts of the human body. Traditional tribal medicines used scarifications in these areas to attract good luck, or for preventive therapy. The jewels worn in these places are never purely aesthetic. They add a magical or a medicinal effect to the ornamentation. Again, a correspondence can be seen here with acupuncture. The research on piercing is in its infancy. As long as it is done hygienically, piercing could be a genuine preventive or curative therapeutic system. It is still too early to specifically establish the best ways to administer and use it.

Rings

A ring worn on the left pinky will radiate its energy all along the arm and target the nose, throat, ears, and everything that concerns the bronchia and lungs. On the fourth (ring) finger of the left hand, the effects will be divided between the circular muscles called sphincters. A stone worn on the left middle finger will affect the cardiovascular system. A ring worn on the left index finger will act directly on mental or psychological problems such as depression, neurosis, and anger. The left thumb is directly connected to sexuality and the reproductive functions.

The effects will be both different and complementary on the right hand. A stone worn on the right pinky will aid clear thinking by healing mental confusion and memory loss. Wearing a ring on the fourth (ring) finger of the right hand will strengthen the inner ear, sense of balance, and receptiveness to outer sensorial stimuli: sight, hearing, touch, smell, taste. The right middle finger relates to skin diseases, and diseases of the nails and hair. The index finger is related to the lymphatic network and infectious problems. Last of all, the right thumb relates to digestion as a whole and the enrichment of the blood through the action of the viscera.

Bracelets Ornamented with Stones

The effects of bracelets made of copper, brass, steel, gold, and silver are well known. To this we can add the effects of stones. The stones' radiance will add to the metal's and affect the energetic pathways and meridians.

Brooches

Some stones, such as amber and pearls, can be tarnished by contact with the skin. Others can be dissolved by perspiration. It's best to wear these stones as a brooch or pin, even if the effect is less potent. These stones can also be applied to the areas concerned or to the corresponding chakras for 20 minutes at a time. If used in this limited way, they won't tarnish or disintegrate.

MODERN SCULPTED STONE SHAPES

Although it may be less common today to find a stone carved in the shape of the organ we wish to treat, shaped stones are still readily available. Balls, pears, and eggs are common shapes and each has its own unique energetic qualities.

Stone Balls

Stone balls are for the home and should not leave one's place of residence. They are the tutelary gods that watch over the home and family. Some stones should be used with precaution. It is better not to let a child play with a stone ball. If a child is strongly attracted, show it to him, allow him to touch and stroke it while you explain its powers in specific terms.

Crystal Ball

The classic crystal ball of the seer and sorcerer is generally made out of leaded glass. It is very rare to find a ball polished from natural rock crystal. In any case, you don't *see* images in a crystal ball as if it's a television screen. The crystal serves to deepen the meditation, reflection, and analysis of the sharp psychologist that a seer always is. The crystal ball can also be used as an inner mirror. It amplifies our psychic perceptions. Meditating while staring at a crystal ball helps us to get in touch with our inner selves. The object's roundness represents the world within. The crystal ball has a balancing effect and will aid any healing we may need.

Hematite Ball

What somber, powerful beauty an iron stone has! And what strength! The object's heaviness both reassures us and makes us uneasy. There is something wild behind this metallic mineral. There's something bitter, too. This stone strengthens the will and makes us relentless. It helps us stand our ground in spite of blows and upsets. It enables us to resist discouragement and maintain our position despite all opposition. Of course, this obstinacy can result in stupid pigheadedness. It's important not to abuse this power.

The metallic brilliance of this ball allows us to see ourselves distorted, as if we were gazing into a fun house mirror. By analyzing our faces, we are likely to discover some of the hidden talents and intimate truths that lurk in the very depths of our souls. The hematite ball reflects, amplifies, and redistributes our psychic energy.

Jade Ball

This ball seems almost timid—too gracious, too delicate. Yet, the green jade ball has a powerful personality. It acts calmly while it neutralizes bad influences and dangerous vibrations. If you love touching it and stroking it, it will blossom and exhale its aura like a precious perfume.

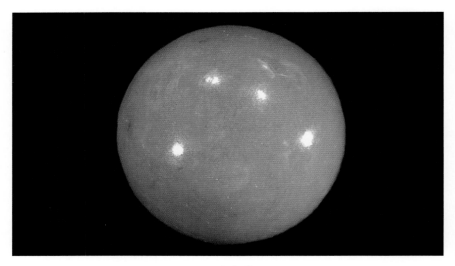

Jade ball

This will result in a feeling of happy fullness in your body. You will feel bigger, and full of compassion and caring.

In spite of its apparent gentleness, the jade ball is one of the rare balls that can counteract the obsidian ball's sometimes devastating power. If you feel too shocked by the latter, touch a jade ball after you've put away the obsidian ball. It's best not to put them in each other's presence—that would create sparks! Slowly, the jade's influence will offer its soft, soothing presence.

Jasper Ball

The jasper ball will help us to keep our feet on the ground. It helps us avoid building castles in the air, and letting ourselves be carried away by a foolish fantasy. If you have a tendency to live with your head in the clouds, green jasper can bring you back down to earth. Red jasper is more energetic, but it can lead to gross materialism. The heliotrope—green jasper spotted with red—is the ideal ball for anyone suffering from weakness or depression.

Lapis Lazuli Ball

The perfect beauty and harmony created by the form and color of this ball has a balancing effect. The lapis lazuli ball looks like sodalite, but it's more powerful. This ball has an inimitable quality, a poetic but active *je-ne-sais-quoi,* which brings the calm, inner peace favorable for well thought-out positive action. The balance gained is favorable for harmonious relations, friendship, and love. It helps us deserve the affection of those close to us and it strengthens our feelings.

Obsidian Ball

The obsidian is a strange stone and it should be handled with care. Its beauty can become poisonous and it can act like a drug, a contraindicated psychotropic.

This stone puts us face to face with our darkest truths, our suppressed inner demons. It turns everything from top to bottom. It plunges us into the "dark night of the soul" where we get in touch with our most ancient anxieties and obsessive fears. The obsidian ball shakes us up, which can be beneficial, but it can also give us a violent, profound shock, and lead us to a state of self-disgust, despair, and melancholy.

As long as you can stand the shock, and accept the idea of questioning your entire existence, you can use the obsidian ball. It shouldn't be left out; when not in use, put it away in a closet and cover it up with cloth made of natural fibers. You can consult this ball from time to time to receive a challenging reality check. Given its profound effects, it's best not to use the obsidian ball more than once every four months. As long as you are able to bear it, this profound inner questioning can be extremely beneficial. Although it can lead unstable minds into certain mental disorders, it can also elevate us to great spiritual heights and realizations.

But take note: you could decide to leave everything behind and take off on a mystical quest, abandoning the people close to you, or you could be swept away by a deep, burning passion.

Orange Calcite Ball

This ball has a very positive effect on those suffering from mental or emotional problems. It will accelerate healing and shorten the convalescence period. Placed near a sick person's bed, it produces an effect that is both gentle and joyous, energetic and serene.

Quartz Ball

The green quartz in the form of a ball symbolizes reasoned hope. This ball does not aid in completing projects. Instead, it helps to highlight work that has already been accomplished. It acts like an advertisement or press release!

The pink quartz ball is both energetic and intimate. It is a symbol of tenderness, of sensual love. It excites creativity before action. It also enhances reflection and meditation and helps us avoid bad ideas and risky adventures. Like all stone balls, it represents the person who gazes at it, who appreciates and loves it. It will also help us to strengthen our self-esteem and be more open to other people's ideas.

Sodalite Ball

The sodalite ball corrects aggressiveness toward others—and ourselves. It can reduce the tendency toward sadism or masochism. Its powerful vibration will help those who have a tendency to express self-justification. An aura of peace emanates from this ball. It helps us open up our third eye. Roll this ball on the Ajna chakra between your eyes. Right away, you'll feel lighter, freer, and more cheerful. This stone ball also encourages deep thoughts and invites spirituality. It strengthens concentration and encourages meditation.

There are many other stone balls, of course, and you can create new ones. Becoming familiar with the minerals will allow you to determine—and appreciate—their properties.

Pear-Shaped Stones

Pears are associated with death in China; the flower of the pear tree is white, the color of mourning in that civilization. In the West, the pear tree is one of the trees that represent nature and human beings. Its hard wood has been used in engraving for centuries. A stone cut in a pear shape has the qualities of a ball made of the same mineral but its effects are reduced. Pears make us aware of our fragility, the fleetingness of existence, and the vagaries of destiny.

Jade Pear

This pear symbolizes hope and destiny and invites us to put our lives in order. By meditating with it, you will understand both the reasons for old animosities, and how to put them to rest. It will enable you to connect with people in your past to better understand them—and yourself.

Jet Pear

This mineral's dark black color mustn't fool us. Jet, combined with this shape, makes people joyous. The black takes on a special vibration of joy that is sometimes tumultuous. By applying the little tip of the pear to the chest, you will feel a strong desire to celebrate—even if you felt depressed beforehand.

It may open the door to overindulgence. Pay attention to your liver and heart. You could also experience some digestive problems and headaches. This stone can help diminish the effects of alcohol consumption but you shouldn't abuse this particular aspect of the jet pear.

Sodalite Pear

This stone helps us to appreciate our real talents. Apply the little tip to your forehead and breathe deeply. Hold your breath for about ten seconds and then let it out slowly. You will experience a new openness that will allow you to see new possibilities.

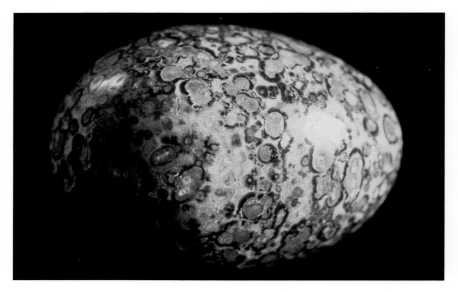

Jasper egg

Stone Eggs

The egg symbolizes both birth and pregnancy. It represents life and direction; the big end of the egg represents the origin and the little one symbolizes direction, destiny, and orientation. Eggs were once used in fortune-telling. An egg was placed on its side on a round table. One person sitting at the table would give it a spin; when it stopped spinning, the little end pointed to the person who was going to die the soonest, the big end to the person who would live the longest.

The egg's energy is oriented toward a single direction. You can touch a painful or diseased area of your body with the small tip. Its action will be precise and almost immediate.

Hematite Egg

This egg profoundly modifies the problems of character. It calms angry people and discourages those who gossip and slander. It also helps those with low self-esteem.

Orange Calcite Egg

In addition to the usual indications for calcite, this egg will help lessen bad moods, depression, and the anger and fear of those suffering from health problems.

Rock Crystal Egg

The rock crystal egg concentrates the qualities of this mineral. Refer to the listing for this crystal in chapter 1.

Rose Quartz Egg

This egg softens spiteful and angry temperaments. It also calms those who have fallacious arguments.

CONTRAINDICATIONS

Focusing on the beauty of a particular stone can cause us to choose a mineral that is not right for us, or one that is not appropriate for our health. For example, a dynamic stone, worn by an obsessive, hyperactive person, could increase her agitation. It could also calm her down, depending on how it is applied. It is necessary to be very careful in your choice and use of stones.

While it is rare for a stone to have a really harmful effect, conditions of sadness, hatred, and self-disgust can come from wearing a contraindicated stone. The most classic case is that of the hypertensive person. Hypertension often affects people with a generous, expansive, and energetic character. This emotional disposition predisposes them to appreciate the powerful brilliance of the red stones set in gold.

Unfortunately, these are exactly the types of stones and metals they should not wear! Hypertension will be exacerbated by these minerals. Very often, all we have to do is stop wearing them for the tension to subside. In some cases of cardiac insufficiency, replacing a person's red jewels—for example, a ruby or garnet set in gold—with blue-green or green stones can help to relieve the disorders. Rhodochrosite, chrysocolla, chrysoprase, hematite, agate, blue topaz, azurite, emerald, and the rare but superb green garnet will calm a hypertensive person. In these cases, it's best to choose silver, titanium, or platinum settings rather than gold, even if it is white.

If you find yourself systematically attracted to stones that do not correspond to you, ask yourself about your relationship with nature, with time, your personal history, and your fears and phobias. This might be the sign of a neurosis with a slight masochistic or sadistic tendency, a state of shock or mourning, or a trauma from childhood that you don't consciously remember. In general, the reason for this attraction is not hard to understand and the appropriate stone, even if you weren't initially attracted to it, can help you to heal.

STONE WATERS AND ELIXIRS

In the ancient world many medicines had a mineral base. Legend has it that Cleopatra, the queen of Egypt, used a solution made from pearls dissolved in vinegar, both as a beauty aid and as medicine for her menstrual disorders. However, this remedy can cause serious gastritis, burning in the stomach, and even ulcers.

The famous "Danzig brandy," dear to the soldiers of eighteenth-century Germany, and sold today in Poland, contains gold sequins. This metal is also used in pharmaceutical preparations. However, the courageous military men of Frederic the Great apparently appreciated the added alcohol more than the curative qualities of this mineral. And of course, the shiny gold sequins in the liquid make an enjoyable spectacle. Brandies were also made with pyrite and silver but the alcohol annihilates the minerals' beneficial effects.

On the other hand, the simple and easy to make stone water is one of the best ways to practice lithotherapy. Stone waters are made by soaking a stone overnight in a bowl of water. (Unless a different amount of time is given for a particular stone in chapter 1.) The water will take on the stone's vibratory and magnetic properties. By drinking it in the morning, you can regenerate yourself or heal a specific health problem.

An even stronger concoction can be made by exposing a bowl to the light of the moon, especially a full moon. A spectacular, but less long-lasting "booster" effect can be obtained by exposing a bowl to the sun for seven hours. The light colored transparent and translucent stones absorb the sunbeams particularly well. Both procedures can produce good results, but they should never be used together with the same water—nor should the two waters ever be mixed. Likewise, two waters prepared with different stones should never be mixed.

It's important to make sure that the stones are perfectly clean and well maintained (see the Gemstone Care and Maintenance chapter). It is also important not to use mineral water. The trace elements of minerals could counteract the effect of the stones. Using distilled, demineralized water will allow the vibratory qualities of each stone to be fully expressed. Also keep in mind that most plants used for medicinal herb teas and infusions contain trace elements, minerals, and metals. It's important to prepare these beverages with neutral water as well.

Stone waters can be even more easily made by using bowls cut out of stones. Alabaster bowls are one example, but be careful; the stone is often artificially colored. The infamous "amethyst bowl" of legends would be very expensive and require a rare stone of an enormous size and weight.

Note: Only make waters out of those stones recommended in chapter 1 and in part 3. It is best to consult a trained medical professional before beginning treatment.

APPLYING STONES
ON THE BODY

An acupuncturist uses needles to stimulate the meridians of the body. An experienced lithotherapist will stimulate the same points with a stone. It is also possible to treat yourself in some cases, using a few simple techniques.

The easiest treatment consists of massaging a painful area with a polished stone.

You can also place the stone on the area that corresponds to a particular illness. For example, you can place a stone on the abdomen for a liver problem. In some cases, you will want to use a bandage to keep the stone in place on the body. It is important to use bandages made with natural fibers. Some bandages are made with synthetic materials charged with static electricity that can counteract the curative potential of the stones. This method can be used to apply stones to the chakras as well.

Another variation is to lightly "prick" the spot to be treated with a natural or cut point of a particular stone. The energy will then be focused directly on the area you want to heal.

Applying Stones on the Chakras

Specific information on using the stones in relation to these energy centers is given in chapter 5 and in the treatment instructions in part 3. When working with the chakras, you can hold the stone in place at the specific point, secure it to the point with a bandage, or massage the area with the stone. The color of each stone used will add to its effects. A transparent or translucent stone can be used like a magnifying glass to direct sunlight on a particular chakra. But be careful, there is the risk of burns. You can also use a lamp or flashlight to truly concentrate the luminous ray of each stone.

POSSIBLE SIDE EFFECTS

The purifying aspect of stones can sometimes create toxic "discharges." This may show up as redness on the skin but it's not serious and will quickly disappear. You may also experience slight nausea or sensations of vertigo that might make you doubt the effectiveness of lithotherapy. On the contrary, this is a manifestation of its power. This effect is comparable to that of homeopathic remedies that at first seem to accentuate the symptoms. It's the sign of our bodies' healthy receptiveness, and it guarantees the success of the cure. This reaction is necessary in many cases and prepares the groundwork for more profound, constructive and curative reactions.

Healing is a dialogue between the mineral energy and our bodies. They must first learn how to harmonize their vibrations and electromagnetic fields, like two musical instruments tuning to each other. Health is finding a stable balance between forces that are both contradictory and complementary. A collaboration between the vibrations of our various atoms makes it possible to maintain our stability.

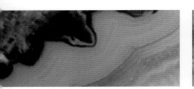

3
GEMS AND CRYSTALS
IN THE HOME

By now we have established that there is a special relationship between human beings and stones. Our bones and teeth consist of minerals that remain even when the vital breath is gone. Our bones support our muscles, but this is not their only role. Our bodies and minds also function like an antenna to receive the multiple waves that the universe sends our way. We are electromagnetic beings and the practice of lithotherapy confirms this fact. But beside their use in treating our illnesses, stones can also benefit us in other ways. The Japanese, for example, organize rock gardens for purposes of contemplation. In our part of the world, we use stones and shells for decoration and some even use ashtrays cut or sculpted from marble and alabaster. This ill treatment of stones still shows our appreciation for their beauty. The presence of stones in the form of balls, decorative sculptures, or other works of art couldn't be more beneficial to our homes.

HOUSES OF STONE
AND STONES IN THE HOUSE

Long before stones decorated our homes they served as our dwelling places; prehistoric caves were our first shelter. Even then, they still had to be hospitable. Archaeologists have discovered caves that were only inhabited for one night; bad vibrations are the likely explanation for the quick abandonment. Some caves, on the other hand, served as shelter for a long time. Hollowed out by nature in more hospitable volcanic tuffs and sandstone, their harmonious energy allowed human life to flourish there.

The word *perron,* meaning "step," is derived from the French word *pierre,* or "stone." The step, the threshold of the house, was often baptized; people poured wine over it and recited incantations. A young bride was carried across the threshold by her husband to symbolize her mastery over the home. This familiarity between the home's female ruler and the entryway stone is rich with symbolism.

In many ancient civilizations, stones were part of the sacred altars that were present in every family dwelling. They were sculpted to resemble the great ancestors or gods. Temples, churches, and other places of worship are built of stones. Many traditions and sacred rituals were passed on to the masons, architects, and project managers of these buildings. These rituals, destined for the "house of God," sometimes spilled over to the workers, too, and they "baptized" or consecrated the new dwellings. Cutting a ribbon to open a new building recalls this practice. The edifice, shelter, or refuge made of stone still has an aspect that connects us to the hidden forces of the world. Even concrete, made up of limestone and silica, preserves this mineral aura.

STONES FOR DAILY USE

Stones are still a necessary part of our everyday lives. They are used to sharpen working tools and culinary utensils. Stone sinks are used for washing and flint is used for lighting fires. However, our daily contact with stones has become more removed. Rather than striking flint against steel, this technology is integrated into lighters. We miss the presence of the primordial stones in our daily lives. Children, who are more receptive to the elementary waves, often bring back pebbles or other stones from a vacation. We sometimes feel intuitively, unconsciously, that we are missing a mineral presence. To find that balance, we can bring stones into our lives that will please us aesthetically and

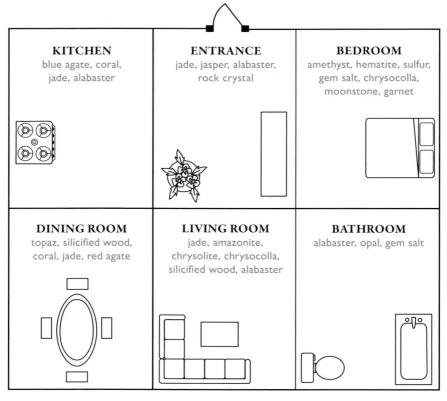

KITCHEN
blue agate, coral, jade, alabaster

ENTRANCE
jade, jasper, alabaster, rock crystal

BEDROOM
amethyst, hematite, sulfur, gem salt, chrysocolla, moonstone, garnet

DINING ROOM
topaz, silicified wood, coral, jade, red agate

LIVING ROOM
jade, amazonite, chrysolite, chrysocolla, silicified wood, alabaster

BATHROOM
alabaster, opal, gem salt

Selected stones for harmony in the home

soothe us with their radiance. Some stones are more suitable than others for a particular room in our homes.

Entrance

The welcoming function of an entrance will be reinforced by the presence of jade, jasper, alabaster, and rock crystal. The ancient Romans placed decorative mosaics there to produce a welcoming effect. However, it's wise not to overload this area with decorations or accessories. It is better to preserve this space's role as a passage or transition between the outside and the personalized interior of a home.

Living Room

A green stone like jade is ideal for a living room, where you want to create a friendly, warm atmosphere.

Amazonite, which is very soothing, calms the mind and can help avoid conflicts caused by heated—or inebriated—conversations. Chrysocolla's peaceful aura, which is livelier than chrysolite, will contribute to an atmosphere of well-being.

Silicified wood harmonizes particularly well with old pieces of furniture and provides a cozy ambience. These silica formations disperse negative waves and mix negative ions in proportion. Moreover, silicified wood, in the company of natural or varnished wood, diminishes the electrical effect of synthetic fibers used in wall-to-wall carpeting and drapes.

Some yellow stones such as alabaster, marble, and other hard limestones can create feelings of both optimism and security. They provide a feeling of warmth, calm, and liveliness that can stimulate the appetite. Moreover, the vibrations emitted through these stones discourage some insects.

In particularly sunny areas, you can use the beautiful blue of azurite, or the deep, dense blue of celestine. Blue, the color of peace, can sometimes tire people out—or put them to sleep. You will want to combine it with other colors in a living room.

Dining Room

A bit more dynamism is welcome in a dining room. Topaz excites the sense of taste; unfortunately, given its cost, it's difficult to use it as decoration. However, you can find impure blocks, or those unsuited for jewelry that can be both pleasing to the eye and a source of beneficial electromagnetic radiance.

Silicified wood, coral, and jade also excite the appetite. This may be the way to bring teenagers addicted to fast food back to the family table. The aura of these stones encourages us to sit down and enjoy the pleasures of the table.

The color red can have the same effect. It's a color that stimulates the appetite—the reason it's used in so many fast-food restaurants. However, this color can incite guests to have lively, animated conversations that turn into arguments. Red's waves need to be tempered with green. Once again, jade can exercise its powerful and peaceful radiance here.

Kitchen

Jade will contribute a feeling of peace to anxious cooks, who are always frightened about ruining a dish. The same is true for the blue-colored stones.

Coral, an energetic mineral, helps to bring meal preparation to completion—sometimes with irritation. An alabaster mortar, used as a decorative object or a kitchen aid, will be welcome here; the slightly euphoric effect of this stone will help you to cook better and prepare inventive, tasty dishes. Last, let us not forget that various stones for sharpening knives also have balancing and grounding qualities.

Bathroom

The bathroom is the place where we take care of ourselves. Alabaster, opal, and all stones that encourage calm and access to our inner life are welcome here. In addition to filing away flaking skin, the pumice stone produces both a gentle and lively radiance. You can refer to the chapter on Astrological Correspondences to personalize your mineral environment in this room.

Bedroom

The bedroom will be the ideal place for amethyst, raw hematite, a beautiful sulfur stone, or a lamp made out of gem salt crystal. These stones enhance sleep.

Chrysocolla, jade, and moonstone will help you to avoid nightmares. Sunstone does this as well, but it may be too invigorating to allow you to get to sleep.

A couple's bedroom will also be enhanced by amazonite, garnet, tourmaline, and the whole range of quartzes. These stones stimulate romantic and sexual activity.

4

GEMSTONE CARE AND MAINTENANCE

As we have seen, stones are energetic entities. One can't say that they are alive in the vegetal or animal sense. But they are born, and they do die. Erosion can cause their physical death. The depletion of their power, which is often noticeable by their dull appearance, represents an energetic, electromagnetic death.

Everything in our world evolves over time. For this process to unfold harmoniously, the natural laws must be respected, and we must feel a sense of communion with the universe. Stones demand our care and respect—and even our affection. They complete us, and an energetic dialogue exists between stones and humans.

A dull or soiled stone should be cleaned. Our aesthetic appreciation of our stones also makes us want to see them shine. Some people use detergent or soap to clean their stones. This is not a good practice; these substances penetrate the mineral pores and can disrupt their vibrations. The use of waxes, even the natural products said to restore luster, is not recommended.

Cleaning stones with salt, vinegar, old wine, or cider is particularly harmful. Also harmful are window cleaning solutions and silver polish. This so-called hygiene shows a lack of respect and concern for the mineral world. Stones only need appreciation and natural substances— water and a tender caress.

The best way to clean your stones is to rinse them with pure water and then gently rub them dry with a fine cotton or linen cloth. The stone will then shine with its own fires. It will light up, recovering its primordial beauty. If a stone comes into contact with a greasy substance (oils, or some types of makeup), dry it carefully. Then powder it with nonperfumed talcum or rich, organic dirt. The delicate sawdust of beech trees, used by watchmakers, will also produce good effects. These powders will absorb the greasy substances and restore the stone's beauty and vibratory power. For stains, use the same procedure. Unfortunately, stains don't always disappear easily on the more porous minerals. However, a natural absorbent powder will reduce the appearance of the stain. It is rare for a stained stone to lose its healing qualities.

HOW TO RECHARGE A STONE

After a lot of use, stones seem to get tired. They become dull and touching them is not as enjoyable. When you try to use them therapeutically, nothing happens. Even worse, they seem to give off a heavy weariness. When that happens, it's time to recharge your stone.

Recharging with Magnetized Needles

After you have washed the stone in water and dried it, place it on a neutral surface such as a wood table or a tablecloth made of a natural fiber. Then take about a dozen pins from a sewing kit and rest them on a magnet. After the pins are magnetized, place them around the stone, pointed toward it, in a clockwise direction. Make sure that each pin is spaced far enough from the others so they will remain in place (despite being magnetized). After about 20 minutes, the stone will respond to the stimulation of the magnetic forces acting in every direction and reactivate its own vibrations.

This procedure is fast acting, but harsh. It quickly recharges the stone, but as a result, the stone will discharge its energy more rapidly making its action short-lived and less effective. In addition, the stone will become tarnished. Nevertheless, in an emergency, you can use this method, as long as you discharge the stone afterward (see page 218), and recharge it again by more gentle means. This procedure will not work with magnetite, magnesium, pyrite, or hematite.

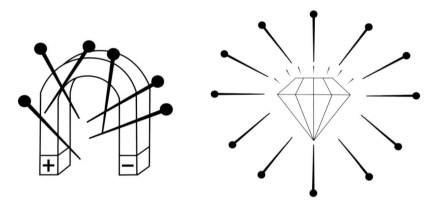

The magnet charging the pins   *The magnetized pins charging the stone*

Contraindicated Method: Recharging with Iron Filings
This procedure consists of burying the stone in magnetized iron filings. This immersion in the iron filings will *kill* a stone. After two or three treatments, the stone will lose all its curative power and become inert.

Using the Elements to Recharge
This is the best procedure by far. It guarantees optimal revitalization and presents no dangers.

Transparent stones need only to be exposed to the sun for a day. Avoid the bright sun and move your stones indoors between the hours of eleven and one o'clock in the afternoon (solar time) so that the strongest rays don't harm or tarnish the stones. You can leave the stones in the sun if you cover them with a white cotton handkerchief. It's important to do this faithfully especially for stones such as amethyst, which contain magnesium. The sun can make their color fade.

Blue and green translucent and opaque stones should be left outside at night during a full moon. The mineral will recover its power by the radiations of this cold light.

Opaque stones can also be recharged by contact with the earth. Wrap the stones in cotton fabric and bury them overnight in a garden or a flowerpot (avoid burying next to cactuses and greasy plants). It has been said that stones buried in this way will "relive their history."

Recharging with Pyramids

The pyramid's geometric shape has mysterious properties. A razor blade will actually become sharp if left for a night in a hollow pyramid under

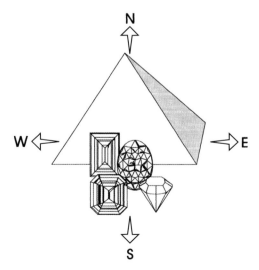

Stones placed under a pyramid, recharging themselves

a full moon. Fruit placed under a pyramid grill will rot much more slowly than usual. Milk curdles less quickly—the reason its first cardboard packaging was in the form of a pyramid.

You can create a pyramid out of light cardboard. Although it is not necessary, you may want to paint the inside of the pyramid with a gouache paint of a complementary color to the stone's. Orient the sides of the pyramid according to the cardinal points and let the stone recharge itself. Avoid aluminum foil or any other metal. They will repel the magnetic forces.

The Twin Crystal Procedure

Stones can also recharge themselves. Place the stone to be recharged near a twin crystal (two crystals with the same crystal lattice points) that has never been used therapeutically. This procedure will also increase the stone's natural energetic power. It's best to place them in an earthenware pot with a cover such as a soup tureen and leave them overnight.

Recharging with Energetic Gongs

This small musical instrument can be found in a metaphysical or music store. Exposing a stone to its sonorous vibrations will tune the gong to the stone's electromagnetic radiance. Mutual stimulation will result, which will reactivate the mineral forces and revive the stone.

HOW TO DISCHARGE OR PURIFY A STONE

At times, a stone can become too charged. It can accumulate an overabundance of negative energy due to our own health problems. Rubbing the stone with a soft cloth doesn't restore its shine. The stone feels heavier and colder than usual. And when you hold the stone in your hand it seems to heat up faster than usual. When this happens, the stone needs to be purified.

To do this, place the stone in a ceramic or wooden bowl filled with demineralized water. Do not use a bowl made of metal, plastic, or stone. Let the stone soak for two days and then dry it gently and thoroughly, using a nonfluffy cloth woven from natural fibers. You may notice bubbles forming around the stone in the water. This indicates that the stone has "worked" a lot and it needs more time to completely discharge the negative energies. Change the water repeatedly until there are no more bubbles. Then let it soak for another week.

Optimal Purification

Some stones need even more purification. This occurs with stones that have been completely saturated with negative energy. This can happen with stones that have been worn during a very serious illness or a period of mourning. The stone may also become charged with its owner's history.

The sad adventure is still told of a member of the French Revolutionary Army who stole the signet ring of an aristocrat sentenced to the guillotine. The ring was ornamented with a very beautiful sapphire, cut in the fashion of the day. After a few days, the thief was affected with an intense buzzing in his ears, nosebleeds, sweating, vertigo, and vision problems. This proud lad, used to booming proclamations and insults, began to stammer. Moreover, he was besieged with nightmares, and his hair turned white in a period of two hours. Soon, deep wrinkles appeared on his forehead and he began to tremble, feel delirious, and suffer from premature dementia. His condition did not originate from remorse. This man, deeply convinced of the necessity of revolutionary violence, was a sincere fanatic. The problem was that the stone, charged with the negative energy of mourning, banishment, and violent death, was producing effects that were opposed to its intrinsic qualities.

Whether this story is true or false—and it's a bit too fanciful to be completely authentic—it nevertheless presents at least a kernel of truth. A stone can be affected by its history. It's important to discharge a stone exposed to negative energy in a particularly scrupulous manner.

To discharge one of these stones, let the stone soak in water for three days and then bury it in the ground. Wrap the stone in thin fabric made of natural fibers so it won't be scratched. Use a bowl containing soil rather than a potted plant. (You don't want the plant to receive all the negative energy contained in the stone.) After three days, dig up the stone. Next, quickly put it through a candle flame. Note: This procedure is not suitable for amber, which might burn. Instead, put amber still wrapped up in linen in the waning sun—only never at noon! Finish off with an "air bath" by placing the stone in a tube open at both ends. You can make a cardboard tube or use a piece of piping made of PVC (a substance made to distribute water in a healthy way). Then place the whole thing outside (on a windowsill, balcony, or in the garden) and orient one end of the tube in the direction of the wind. An air current will form inside the tube, and the stone will be purified by the four elements. Now all that's left is to recharge it.

STORING THE STONES

Using a chest or a small jewelry case are the worst possible ways to store your minerals. Besides the fact that they scratch each other, the curative qualities of each stone's ray can be opposed or modified by the energies of the other stones.

The best solution is to wrap each stone in fine linen and store them in individual cases or simple boxes. The necklaces and bracelets can be hung as long as you leave a space of at least two inches between them. Rings can be slipped onto a wooden rod covered in natural velvet, as long as you leave the same distance between them, and group them together by color, if possible. A wooden, porcelain, or plastic hand might be decorative, but they're not recommended. Jeweler's drawers padded with soft fabric are ideal for storing stones. These professional accessories are made very carefully and, unfortunately, they are very expensive.

PART TWO

Gemstone Correspondences with the Chakras, Colors, and Signs of the Zodiac

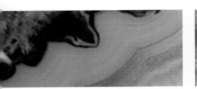

5

HARMONIZATION WITH THE CHAKRAS

The term *chakra,* a Sanskrit word meaning "wheel," has both multiple and complementary meanings. Each meaning responds symbolically to the others, which allows for different levels of study and interpretation. We will only cite a few of them here. An exhaustive study of all the meanings and their correspondences could occupy an entire life.

The seven chakras are located along the spinal column from the base of the spine to the top of the head. Each chakra corresponds to a particular set of nerves and organs in the physical body.

The chakras are not only energy centers or "little suns," they are also energy distributors, whirlwinds of force that make it possible to have energy from the higher planes circulating throughout our bodies.

Their simple, disklike shape recalls the sun with its power and energy. This disk also represents the wheel of destiny and the signs of the zodiac. The chakras respond to color and the therapeutic qualities of the stones. This relation is based both on the laws of physics and those of the higher planes of awareness.

IN SEARCH OF
OUR LOST ENERGY

The chakras also correspond to Vishnu's magical weapon, an eight-ray wheel that "destroys enemies like lightning." These enemies symbolically represent adversity, the physiological or psychological disorders the human body and soul are confronted with during life on Earth. These illnesses and infections drain our energy and make us more and more sensitive. First we accumulate "bruises," and then more serious ailments. As a result, our personalities become gloomy and depressed or spiteful and angry.

Keep in mind that psychological and physical problems respond to and exacerbate one another; depression can lead to alcoholism, liver, or cardiovascular ailments. Sadness, anger, and worry can make us feel desperate. How much of our energy is lost! How much unhappiness there is!

An elementary knowledge of the chakras and the stones that correspond to them can help us to lead more harmonious lives and avoid many misfortunes. This happens by discovering our own sense of balance. Harmony is not an isolated phenomenon; it is a matter of recovering our communion with the earth and the primordial powers. The gradual awakening of the chakras through the process of spiritual development frees our inner energy, which is represented in the mythology of India by the kundalini snake whose latent power lies curled at the base of our spines.

Kundalini is light, sound, and music—a rainbow that resonates with the cosmos. This serpent represents desire and fertility, a positive, creative force, in both the literal and metaphorical sense. By eventually rising up, from chakra to chakra, the kundalini snake drinks and feeds itself with intense, musical energy; each chakra also corresponds to a note on the musical scale. At the start, kundalini represents the female energy, or *shakti*. During its long, slow journey, it will achieve a synthesis of the male and female energetic potentials.

LEARNING THE CHAKRAS

Of course we can study the chakras the way we prepare for a test—by memorizing their location; their effects; and the stone, color, and sign of the zodiac to which each corresponds. We could recite the list like a parrot. However, this is not the best way to prepare for balance. We need time, attention, calm, and even a certain tenderness with ourselves. We need to get in touch with the beneficial forces alive in each of us. It would be better to first get to know one or two chakras, rather than experience difficulties in trying to know all of them all at once.

Step One:
Preparing the Body

Find a quiet place where you're not likely to be disturbed. Next, find a comfortable position: lying down, sitting cross-legged, or standing. Of course, yoga positions are best, but, for the moment, the most important thing is to feel relaxed. So we will not try to imitate a posture from a manual that might knot up our muscles and prevent us from experiencing the sensation of each chakra. The postures are effective and useful, but they require training.

Take off your shoes and wear loose, comfortable clothing. Your clothes should be of one color only. It's best to wear clothes made of wool, cotton, or natural fibers because many synthetic materials have electrostatic properties that can interfere with the circulation of the body's energy currents. A carpeted floor or rug made out of these fibers can cause the same difficulties.

Step Two:
Creating an Environment Conducive to Inner Serenity

Light incense or candles and play gentle, calming music. Be aware that certain electronic devices such as CD players, or radios, emit rays that can interfere with the energy currents of our bodies. If you are especially sensitive, it is better to do without these devices and simply enjoy the silence.

Step Three:
Enhancing the Meditative State

If you haven't practiced abdominal breathing, it may take some time to learn how to breathe differently. Start by breathing slowly and calmly.

To harmonize the chakras, it is also essential to know what meditation is. Many people believe that meditation is a serious, religious practice demanding concentration and arduous efforts. That's not the case. Actually, meditation is quite simply a state of being. When the mind is trained to focus on an outside or inside point long enough to eliminate all distractions, when you can let your thoughts flow without interruption in a single direction, or by concentrating your thoughts on a specific theme, you've arrived at a meditative state.

You may want to begin by visualizing a golden sun above your head, a sun with rays that penetrate your body. To open even more, close your eyes and try to remember a sweet, calm, and happy moment in your past. Practice by evoking this pleasant memory and letting everything else fall away.

We are now ready to study and understand the chakras, without rushing things, so that we will know them deeply, with our hearts and minds, bodies and souls.

We will learn that each chakra corresponds to certain organs, colors, and stones. However, we must not forget that body, mind, and spirit forms the whole. The same is true for the chakras, which correspond and "communicate" with one another. Some of them relate more specifically to a particular organ, but all of them play their role in the interaction of our entire beings. We must not lose sight of that fact, despite the need to study them one by one.

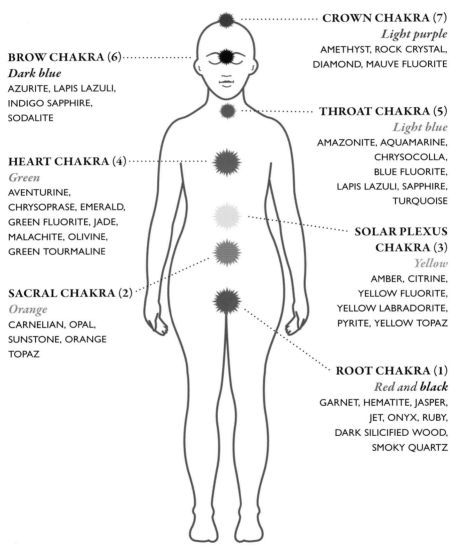

CROWN CHAKRA (7)
Light purple
AMETHYST, ROCK CRYSTAL,
DIAMOND, MAUVE FLUORITE

BROW CHAKRA (6)
Dark blue
AZURITE, LAPIS LAZULI,
INDIGO SAPPHIRE,
SODALITE

THROAT CHAKRA (5)
Light blue
AMAZONITE, AQUAMARINE,
CHRYSOCOLLA,
BLUE FLUORITE,
LAPIS LAZULI, SAPPHIRE,
TURQUOISE

HEART CHAKRA (4)
Green
AVENTURINE,
CHRYSOPRASE, EMERALD,
GREEN FLUORITE, JADE,
MALACHITE, OLIVINE,
GREEN TOURMALINE

**SOLAR PLEXUS
CHAKRA** (3)
Yellow
AMBER, CITRINE,
YELLOW FLUORITE,
YELLOW LABRADORITE,
PYRITE, YELLOW TOPAZ

SACRAL CHAKRA (2)
Orange
CARNELIAN, OPAL,
SUNSTONE, ORANGE
TOPAZ

ROOT CHAKRA (1)
*Red and **black***
GARNET, HEMATITE, JASPER,
JET, ONYX, RUBY,
DARK SILICIFIED WOOD,
SMOKY QUARTZ

*The seven major chakras and their correspondence
with the colors and the stones*

FIRST: MULADHARA/ ROOT CHAKRA

Location: Perineum, base of the spine

Corresponding organs/glands: Suprarenal glands, colon, rectum

Main colors: Red, black

Secondary colors: Blue-green, white

Stones: Garnet, hematite, jasper, jet, onyx, ruby, dark silicified wood, smoky quartz

Energetic aura: Survival, earthly solidity, taking root

Shape: Square

Number: 4

Element: Earth

Sound: *Lam,* sung on the first note of our easiest scale, the middle C, found in the middle of a piano keyboard

Psychological problems and disorders connected to an imbalance in this chakra: Insecurity, instability, distraction, problems with concentration and memory, anorexia, irrational fear, nightmares

Physiological problems and disorders: Muscle cramps in the feet and legs, incontinence, hemorrhoids, varicose veins, cystitis, fibroids, ailments of the intestines, infectious colitis, inflammation of the rectum

---

◇

The first chakra is located at the base of the spine. This chakra is the root, and it is here that the energetic snake lies. The first chakra is elementary; it unites us with the earth, our primitive or animal awareness.

Close your eyes and imagine a disk located at the base of your spine, radiating its light. This energy relates to the suprarenal glands, which are located on the kidneys. Feel the energy coming from the perineum and being exhaled like a fluid or perfume to the kidney area.

This golden or phosphorescent disk, this electrical force, corresponds to two main colors, red and black. It also corresponds to stones of the same colors: garnet, onyx, jade, hematite, ruby, obsidian, and red jasper. Mentally combine and imagine placing these stones on the disk. Later, when you have learned the chakras, you will actually place a stone on the chakra that corresponds to the area you want to heal. The location of this chakra designates the organs it can heal: kidney and urinary infections, and problems related to our legs and feet. (See part 3, Treatment for Specific Conditions.) This mental exercise will prepare you to practice these cures more effectively.

This first chakra is, in fact, the chakra for concentration. It aids concentration at the same time as it heals what prevents it: anger, jealousy, mistrust, and other negative attitudes. Don't worry if you didn't "feel" anything. You're knocking on the right door. Keep practicing this exercise wherever you are—whether it's in the subway or at work. If it doesn't seem to "work," don't worry. Just continue to feel the first chakra: shiny, radiating with its stones and colors. Connect it in spirit with the disturbances you want to heal.

Is there mistrust? Negative attitudes? These lead to disgust with ourselves and others. This chakra also fights the lack of vital appetite and its most common form, anorexia. This sad condition stems from difficulty in communicating and reaching out to others.

Keep visualizing this chakra until you feel familiar with it. Once you have "felt" this chakra, you can embody the square—the elementary symbol of matter. The square represents the earth, poetically, as our living space or shelter. Next, meditate on the symbolism of the number four, as you imagine or know it. To end the meditation, pronounce the sound *lam* several times, from below the stomach; imagine the sound coming from the chakra itself. This "air column" exercise corresponds to the preparatory work that singers do and it helps us to better perceive our own bodies. If you get bored or tired, stop the exercise.

The Etheric Body

We have just met up with our etheric body, the underlying energetic structure of the physical body, our physical body's subtle counterpoint.

The etheric body, sometimes called the vital body, is a web or network of energy currents that travel throughout our system and connect one chakra to the next. We cannot see the current produced by an electric battery and the same thing is true for our own organism. Each chakra can be compared to a battery, and the energetic flow between them constitutes our vital force.

SECOND: SVADHISTHANA/ SACRAL CHAKRA

Location: Lower abdomen, genital organs

Corresponding organs/glands: Womb, ovaries, vagina, prostate, testicles, penis

Main colors: Orange, orangey-red

Secondary colors: Blue, blue-green

Stones: Carnelian, opal, sunstone, orange topaz, all orange-colored stones

Energetic aura: Sexual and reproductive energy, harmony of the male and female polarities, yin/yang balance, intimate relationships

Shape: Crescent-shaped Moon

Number: 6

Element: Water

Sound: *Vam,* to be spoken on the second note of our easiest scale, for example D

Psychological problems and disorders resulting from an imbalance in this chakra: Mistrust, paranoia, and persecution fears; difficulties in relationships; insensitivity to the suffering of others; cruelty, sadism in the most serious cases; erotomania; nymphomania

Physiological problems and disorders: lower back pain, infertility, impotence, frigidity, low libido, menstrual pains

We know our bodies are made of flesh, muscles and bones, organs and nerves. We can even see it with the aid of an X-ray or sonogram. But

our bodies are also vehicles of desire, sexual instinct, and reproductive energy.

This brings us to the second chakra, the one often called the chakra of sex and sexuality. We will first consider it from the point of view of the etheric body, remaining temporarily in the domain of sensation. Desire is a component of love, and here our sexuality takes root, in the very heart of our being and primal emotions.

The second chakra's physical correspondence is the genital organs. This is the chakra of intimate communion and human warmth; in our electromagnetic aura it appears predominantly orange in color.

This is the chakra of communion, which can present itself in the form of a sexual relationship—but not only that. The energy of the blue, secondary color indicates caring and compassionate relations with others. Through the properties of the secondary color, this chakra is mainly connected to two other chakras: the fifth, which is light blue in color, and the sixth, which is dark blue.

To create a treatment for sexual disorders, you will start with the orange stones that address these problems directly. You will then add the complementary blue stones to complete the action of the orange stones. In any case, a problem of a sexual nature is, like all problems, the result or the cause of other unpleasant troubles. It is advisable to treat it in relation to its cause and effects.

Visualize your sexual organ and feel it from the inside. Its erotic role is obvious. However, it is more complete than we imagine. With the sexual act, there is first an energy transfer, a reciprocal gift. The pleasure is also "electrified." Its radiance spreads throughout the body and toward the other chakras.

Meditation on the number 6 (2 × 3) constitutes a double of the female principle represented by the 3. By connecting with this chakra, we begin the fusion, the bringing together of principles. The corresponding sound is harsher; from the low of the first chakra, to the high of the second, sometimes coming back to the sound of the Muladhara chakra.

Desire and pleasure offer a general radiance that is not limited to the sexual level. A blockage in this area deeply disturbs and harms us on many levels. An imbalance makes us spiteful and agitated, and we experience bitterness, rancor, and self-disgust. The corresponding stones and colors act on this chakra to free us from these disorders and the obsessive fears they create.

The Astral Body

Here, we are in sync with our emotional or astral body. Its energy, superimposed on that of our physical bodies, enriches our sensations. It builds our personality, our individuality. As its name indicates, it is in direct relation with the planets, the stars, and the signs of the zodiac. It is a bridge between the emotions and physical matter.

THIRD: MANIPURA/ SOLAR PLEXUS CHAKRA

Location: Navel to solar plexus

Corresponding organs: Stomach, pancreas, liver, gallbladder

Main color: Yellow

Secondary color: Purple

Stones: Amber, citrine, yellow fluorite, yellow labradorite, pyrite, topaz, and other yellow stones

Energetic aura: Will, solidarity, digestion, determination

Shape: Triangle

Number: 10

Element: Fire

Sound: *Ram,* to be sung on the note E, or the third note of the scale

Psychological problems and disorders resulting from imbalance of this chakra: Anger, fear, futility, anxiety, obsession, repetitive compulsions, a quick temper, lack of self-confidence

Physiological problems and disorders: Digestion problems, ulcers, diabetes, hypo- or hyperglycemia, eating disorders, heavy sweating

Located above the navel, this chakra corresponds to the *ki* of Zen. It is the chakra of the will, of individual power. But we have to understand the nature of will. We can keep repeating to ourselves *"I want this or that"* and force ourselves to take aggressive action. We will no doubt

get what we want. Even so, it's better to be relaxed. Will is initiatory. Once we are clear about what we want to manifest, we need to let go. One way to make this apparent paradox understandable is to think of the practice of archery. The archer must first have the desire to hit the target, then aim, draw the bow, and let the arrow go. The archer might identify himself with the arrow, but he is not the arrow. He must let it find the target on its own; he is no longer controlling the action.

The will functions in the same way: we can create the initial energy and put things in motion. But then we must let go. This requires a certain sureness within ourselves exempt of the pride that would ruin everything—and harm the psyche as a result. The will, in all its purity, also demands our inner honesty. When we feel safe within, we are more likely to control our aggressiveness and avoid conflict and power struggles with others.

This is also the chakra of emotion and instinct. The "gut feelings" that often guide our daily lives are centered in this region. This chakra is activated by our deep attachment to family and friends. It is also active when we fall in love. We carry our worries and emotional baggage here—fear that can cause knots in our stomachs and other emotions that can "turn our stomachs inside out."

To get in touch with this chakra, visualize a light yellow disk. It will help to think of the archer's arrow surging from your solar plexus like a shooting ray of light. The shape of this chakra is different from that of the first chakra, which expands and snakes around like the roots of an oak tree, or that of the more immaterial second chakra that radiates its electric energy like the heat of a frying pan. The effect of a stone placed on the solar plexus chakra will be incisive, rapid, precise, and sometimes even immediate.

Proceed by meditating on the number 10, the triangle, and the element of fire. Say *ram* on all the notes—this can be very gentle and swell to a rough sound.

The Mental Body

The mental body concerns the intellectual—rumination and reflection that lead to intimate self-knowledge. Once we've nourished ourselves with meditation, vision, and knowledge, this energy lives in us and strengthens us.

FOURTH: ANAHATA/ HEART CHAKRA

Location: Heart

Corresponding organ/gland: Heart, thymus

Main colors: Green, pink, gold

Secondary color: None

Stones: Aventurine, chrysoprase, emerald, green fluorite, jade, malachite, olivine, green tourmaline

Energetic aura: Love, human and divine; self-esteem and esteem for others

Shape: Six-pointed star (two interlaced triangles)

Number: 12

Element: Air

Sound: *Yam,* to be sung on the fourth note of the scale, F, for example. Try to feel its stature as a subdominant note, strongly drawn by the upper note and close to the one that precedes it, a half-tone away.

Psychological problems and disorders resulting from an imbalance of this chakra: Sadness, loneliness, selfishness, mood instability, bitterness, self-denigration, and denigrating others

Physiological problems and disorders: Cardiac and cardiovascular problems, poor circulation, rashes, hives, boils, shingles, disturbances of arterial tension, buzzing in the ears

We have arrived at the fourth chakra, the first chakra located above the diaphragm. We have now crossed the boundary between the personal

and the universal. The lower chakras represent our animal nature and instincts. As we cross the boundary of the diaphragm, we take our first steps into the spiritual realm. Below the diaphragm, our consciousness is centered on "me." Above the diaphragm, we move into the universal consciousness of "we."

The heart, the symbol of the fourth chakra, has a double, complementary significance in most languages. Like the tongue, which is both an organ and a means of communication, the heart is an organ, the vital pump that distributes blood throughout our bodies. It is also the symbol of love and courage.

This muscle, with its involuntary contractions, beats the cadence of our emotions. Its double emotional and physical nature is obvious— when we are in love, our hearts "skip a beat," and the loss of love "breaks our hearts." The heart also relates to the unconditional love and compassion exemplified by Jesus—a universal love that encompasses all of creation. The beating heart is the eternal vibration of love.

This valiant organ gives rhythm to our lives. The heart's regularity stimulates healing and restores our equilibrium. It also stimulates us to enjoy beauty. This chakra relates both to our aesthetic sense, and our creative joy.

The energy of the fourth chakra is expressed in waves, like the harmonics accompanying the sound of a bell or gong, or the ripples in the water when pebbles are thrown into a lake. A stone placed on this chakra will radiate in the same way, extending the force of its healing energy throughout the entire body.

The heart chakra's green energy responds to the yellow that precedes it. It has no complementary color. Pink and green express the profound energy of love, which the color gold enhances. Visualize these colors, and give them the vibration of love.

The triangle, the air, the number twelve . . . let your spirit wander as you enjoy these images. The *yam* sound is tender; feel the pleasure of unconditional love.

FIFTH: VISHUDDHA/ THROAT CHAKRA

Location: Throat, larynx, upper part of the lungs, ears, nose

Corresponding organ/gland: Thyroid, lungs

Main color: Light blue

Secondary color: Orange (but not too intense)

Stones: Amazonite, aquamarine, chrysocolla, blue fluorite, lapis lazuli, sapphire, turquoise

Energetic aura: Communication and creativity

Shape: Triangle pointed downward

Number: 16

Element: Ether

Sound: *Ham,* to be pronounced strongly, joyously on the note G, the dominant note, the clear sound at five degrees from the initial C, a sound of victory that can become thunderous

Psychological problems and disorders resulting from the imbalance of this chakra: Blocked creativity, stammering, inability to speak up, a voice that is feeble, flat, or quavering

Physiological problems and disorders: Thyroid problems, lung disease, asthma, chronic colds and throat infections, sinus problems, stiff necks

We now arrive at a chakra that concerns communication and creativity. The first sign of equilibrium in this chakra is the voice.

Voices sometimes lose their clarity and nodules can form on the vocal cords, making the voice unpleasantly raspy. This phenomenon is becoming more and more frequent, and speech therapists are now in high demand. Before this problem starts, you can meditate on the fifth chakra, and begin lithotherapy with the corresponding stones.

Our voices also change with age, and the voices of old people are often thought to be less pleasing than those of the young. Lithotherapy will slow down or even eliminate this process and make it possible to preserve a vital, pleasant-sounding voice.

Communication is a creative process and creativity is also important to the equilibrium of this chakra. Communication can take many forms. We can communicate through words by speaking, or by writing books, articles, or poetry. We can also express our creativity through the visual arts in the form of drawing, painting, or sculpting. Music and dance are also ways to communicate and express ourselves creatively.

You can balance this chakra energetically by imagining a triangle connecting the fifth, second, and third chakras. You can also "walk" the sound *ham* from one chakra to the next by breathing out the *h* sound forcefully.

SIXTH: AJNA/BROW OR THIRD EYE CHAKRA

Location: Between the eyebrows and behind the skull, at the same height

Corresponding organ/gland: Eyes, pituitary gland

Main color: Dark blue

Secondary colors: Deep red-orange, fluorescent orange

Stones: Azurite, lapis lazuli, indigo sapphire, sodalite

Energetic aura: Intuition, stimulation, and development of the extra-sensory powers

Shape: No special shape. If need be, the circle or disk representing the third eye

Number: 2

Element: None, or all

Sound: *Om* or *aum,* to be said aloud on a note of A or B, or even B flat

Psychological problems and disorders resulting from the imbalance of this chakra: Distraction, hypersensitivity, concentration difficulties, feeling "spaced out," hallucinations, vertigo

Physiological problems and disorders: Blindness, eye strain, blurred vision, facial neuralgia, headaches, nightmares, buzzing in the ears, mental confusion, problems with balance, and problems in the central nervous system

With this chakra we enter the realm of the subtle world—the world beyond the reach of our five senses. We do not develop our perceptual skills overnight. However, by meditating on this chakra, we can strengthen our intuition and increase our sensitivity to the higher planes.

Meditation is especially important at this stage of our spiritual journey. To enter the higher worlds of peace and wisdom, we must learn to quiet our minds and tame our unruly emotions. A mind as serene as a still pond is the goal.

Say *om* or *aum* out loud, on a note of A, B, or B flat. The "basic" vibration of A, the one that serves as a standard for tuning, is drawn upward by the seventh note between B natural and B flat. Try it, even if you don't sing on pitch.

The infamous sound *om* will reveal its power to you. First, say it internally. Then "push" the sound, until it gets to the surface and comes out of your throat. There is an equivalent sound in the Christian tradition—the Ave Maria said very quickly in Latin—which the medieval monks in the eighteenth century used in their meditation.

The fact that two very different religious traditions used a similar sound with the goal of elevating the soul shouldn't surprise us, for many other correspondences exist. Om or aum, which means "the beginning and the end" in Sanskrit, is analogous to the Christian alpha and omega.

Now we can recapitulate the sounds. Try to sing successively the notes and syllables that correspond both to the chakra you want to heal and its complementary chakras. The vibrations of your voice will hasten the healing of any illnesses or disorders.

SEVENTH: SAHASRARA/ CROWN CHAKRA

Location: Top of the head

Corresponding organ/gland: Cerebral cortex, pineal gland

Main colors: Mauve, purple, white

Secondary colors: Yellow, black

Stones: Amethyst, rock crystal, diamond, mauve fluorite

Energetic aura: Eternity, intuition, the soul, knowledge of the cosmos

Shape: No particular shape

Number: 100 and/or 1,000

Element: None, or all

Sound: Silence

Psychological problems and disorders resulting from the imbalance of this chakra: Hypersensitivity, alienation, confusion, concentration problems, insomnia, hallucinations, vertigo

Physiological problems and disorders: Brain disorders, migraines, trouble with balance

———————————— ◇ ————————————

The crown chakra is called the "thousand-petaled lotus," or the *brahmarandra* in India. When we reach this stage, the consciousness has matured, and the fusion of ego and spirit is complete.

We are now solidly connected to the cosmos. The "infinite silences" of space and time are within our grasp. We are in a state of grace and our radiance has a beneficial influence on those around us. The mystical intoxication of the color mauve (see Amethyst) no longer carries a risk. Mauve gently accelerates this fusion between man and the supernatural world.

The will, represented by the third chakra, and the complementary color yellow, will balance the power of this chakra. The spirit is still rooted in matter, and we, at last, live with "our head in the clouds, and our feet on the ground."

The Spiritual Body

The spiritual or causal body is often called "the temple of the soul." It is the divine storehouse where the sum of our experiences, life after life, are stored. This body is referred to in the Bible as the "house not made with hands, eternal in the heavens" (2 Cor. 5:1). This soul body allows us to retain and carry forward the wisdom gained in each lifetime.

The spiritual body reigns over the etheric and astral bodies. To feel it, you have to imagine its energy in waves. With a disciplined meditation practice, we can eventually contact this body—and its wisdom—at will.

6

THE LANGUAGE
OF COLORS

An energy-bearing ray, color has therapeutic power. Each color corresponds to a particular pathology.

The light's radiance is more or less absorbed by matter. White repels all rays, and black absorbs them totally. The intermediary colors absorb some frequencies and repel others. These luminous rays correspond to the body's rays and they vibrate—or don't vibrate—with it. As we have seen, this harmonization of the frequencies is the main basis for the power of minerals.

Some radiations are too powerful for some people. For this reason you will use stones with a complementary color to balance or temper an effect that's too strong. (Refer to the end of this chapter for more information on using the complementary colors.)

RED STONES

Red, the color of blood, evokes energy. The red stones are full of material force. This color is the color of power, from the crimson of the noble Romans, to the simple red light that halts traffic. Red's authority is incontestable. It is also the color chosen to excite bulls during a bullfight.

To varying degrees, the red stones heal energetic deficits, whether it manifests as heart insufficiency or problems with breathing. However, the implacable nature of the color red can also produce anxiety.

Red stones, such as ruby, coral, and garnet show us dazzling variations of color that correspond to the quantity of vibrations absorbed. The deeper the red, the more the stone is "charged" with rays. However, light rubies, once they are cut, add to these properties the qualities of the luminous rays that rebound and strengthen the other facets.

Complementary colors: blue-green and green

ORANGE STONES

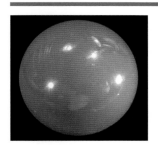

The orange stones include carnelian, sunstone, and certain corals. This color predisposes people to action without generating anxiety. It can correct the too dreamy temperament of those who have their heads "in the clouds."

Complementary color: blue

YELLOW STONES

The yellow stones include citrine, sulfur, amber, and topaz. Yellow represents vitality and basic heat. It protects and gives a sense of security. Its positive power encourages both action, and its complement, active meditation.

Complementary color: purple

YELLOW-GREEN STONES

These stones include moldavite, chrysoprase, and pale jade. This is the color of springtime and renewal, the time of year when nature comes back to life after the long months of winter. Yellow-green energy predisposes us to fast healing and prepares us for the deeper action of the deep green stones.

Complementary color: mauve

GREEN STONES

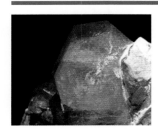

The green stones include olivine, green fluorite, malachite, and emerald. Green is the color of fertility, fecundity, and natural balance. It is a color of hope. Green stones radiate a calm and restful energy.

Complementary colors: red, orange, according to the intensity

BLUE-GREEN STONES

The blue-green stones include amazonite, chrysocolla, turquoise, and aquamarine. This color stimulates relaxed concentration and helps us balance our passions and emotions. It is also the color of friendship.

Complementary color: red

BLUE STONES

These stones include lapis lazuli, azurite, sapphire, and sodalite. Blue is not only the color of the sky, it is also the color of the forget-me-not flower. The radiations of the blue stones fortify the intellect. This elevation encourages science, knowledge, even peace.

Complementary color: orange

MAUVE AND PURPLE STONES

These stones include amethyst, ametrine, and fluorite. The colors of spirituality and religion, mauve and purple differ only by the number of frequencies absorbed or rejected. Purple offers a purer, more "targeted" energy than mauve, which gives off a more diffuse strength. The spirituality inherent in this color can draw us to mysticism—or fanaticism. It may be useful to wear a complementary color at the same time.

Complementary colors: yellow-green and yellow

WHITE OR TRANSPARENT STONES

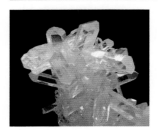

These stones include alabaster, diamond, and rock crystal. They help us reconnect with the inner self that can get lost in the day-to-day grind of modern life. This sometimes unbearable clarity and purity can cause us to judge ourselves harshly. Watch out for the tendency to become ungrounded or to mistrust the body.

Complementary colors: all of them to various degrees

BLACK STONES

The black stones include obsidian, magnetite, onyx, and jet. They represent the earth and its implacable force, the underlying fire. This color puts us in touch with our inner truths but the revelation it brings can lead to depression.

Complementary color: white

THE COMPLEMENTARY COLORS

The balance between a stone of one color and the stone in its complementary color makes it possible to compensate for both the particular effects of each stone and the excesses of certain temperaments in each of us.

An angry person, with excessive "red" qualities, whose temperament makes him unbearable to be around, will be soothed by wearing a green or blue-green stone, depending on the severity of the imbalance.

On the advice of mental health professionals, the walls of most American prisons are painted blue or blue-green. This color has noticeably reduced the number of scuffles and fights so frequent in these penitentiaries. Likewise, in care units reserved for people with depression or alcoholics going through detoxification, walls painted orange have given back a bit of the joy of life to these unhappy patients.

When combining stones, the stone of the complementary color should be noticeably smaller than the primary stone.

7
ASTROLOGICAL CORRESPONDENCES

The correspondence between the stones and the constellations is both obvious and subtle. For example, the combination of jasper with Cancer is well known to most astrologers.

But beyond the obvious affinities, you will discover a stronger degree of resonance between the stones and the signs if you take the time to meditate. With a little attention and concentration, you will discover the special universe of connection and harmony between the two.

The stones associated with the signs listed here do not necessarily have a curative or a medical function. Instead, it is a general affinity that creates a harmonious relationship between the planets and their terrestrial sisters, the stones. It goes without saying that we can only give general correspondences. They will be refined, and sometimes contradicted, by knowledge of the ascendants (rising signs). Even so, there are general rules that make it possible to see the basic relationship between the stones and the signs.

You will find it helpful to refer back to chapter 1, Directory of Gems and Crystals, to review the general characteristics and therapeutic qualities of the stones corresponding to a given sign.

PISCES
Amethyst
Coral
Labradorite
Olivine

ARIES
Carnelian
Red jasper
Ruby

TAURUS
Emerald
Lapis lazuli
Rose quartz
Blue sapphire

AQUARIUS
Aquamarine
Falcon's eye
Fluorite
Turquoise

CAPRICORN
Chalcedony
Emerald
Obsidian
Onyx

GEMINI
Chalcedony
Citrine
Tiger's eye
Golden topaz

SAGITTARIUS
Amethyst
Lapis lazuli
Blue sapphire
Turquoise

CANCER
Emerald
Labradorite
Moonstone
Opal

SCORPIO
Garnet
Jet
Onyx

LEO
Amber
Citrine
Rock crystal
Diamond
Olivine

LIBRA
Chrysocolla
Smoky quartz
Golden topaz

VIRGO
Yellow agate
Carnelian
Jasper
Yellow sapphire

The twelve signs of the zodiac
and selected stone correspondences

ARIES

March 21–April 20 • Element: Fire • Ruling planet: Mars

 This sign represents springtime and rebirth. One of the royal fire signs, the Aries people are natural born leaders. Ruled by Mars, they are assertive, aggressive, and willful. Self-assured and confident, they frequently find themselves in positions of authority.

Amethyst: This stone will help those born under the sign of Aries to avoid being carried off suddenly by their moods and whims. The amethyst will temper the ruby's action and give them greater access to their inner self.

Red carnelian: There is harmony and complicity between this stone and the sign of Aries. A stone of enterprise, a carnelian will inspire natives of this sign to launch new projects.

Coral: Paradoxically, this marine mineral will allow Aries natives to feel more grounded and rooted in the earth. It will help them to accept who they are, and to realize that they can grow and change.

Diamond: The diamond will confront Aries with his destiny. A stone of great purity, the diamond will usher in a period of contemplation and rebirth.

Garnet: This stone has the same qualities as the ruby. But, in focusing the creative power of those born under the sign of Aries, the garnet will add patience, perseverance, and attention to others. It will even open them to new points of view.

Hematite: This stone's metallic brilliance is in tune with the Aries spirit and will strengthen the determination to fulfill ambitions.

Red jasper: Aries' impetuousness will be tempered and balanced by these stones. Jasper will also help those born under this sign to be more caring and wise in their relationships with others.

Ruby: For all lords, all honors! Rubies evoke the power of the ram, a power that is sometimes overbearing and needs to be channeled constructively. Aries natives must be careful with this stone. The red can exacerbate their natural aggressiveness. For those who have a tendency to lose their temper, it's important not to wear this stone every day.

Other good stones for those born under the sign of Aries include: amazonite, ametrine, chrysolite, heliotrope, iolite, jasper, opal, peridot, magnetite, sunstone, red tanzanite, and tourmaline.

TAURUS

April 21–May 20 • Element: Earth • Ruling planet: Venus

 Taurus represents the earthly forces of fertility, germination, and fecundation. While Taurus natives are generally sweet natured and friendly, they can also be very direct and impatient. Those born under this sign are especially fond of nature, and the sensuous pleasures of romance and sexuality.

Agate: Taurus has a tendency to blindly charge forward. This is often due to fear and a lack of self-confidence. This earthy stone will bring Taurus a satisfying feeling of stability and security.

Chalcedony: One of the Taurus native's weak points is a lack of tolerance and the tendency to dictate to others. Chalcedony will help those born under this sign to accept and appreciate the ideas of others. It will also help them let go of the need to always be right.

Chrysocolla: This stone encourages compassion and inner peace. Chrysocolla will help Taurus slow down and look within. This sign has a spiritual potential that is often overshadowed by practical concerns. Chrysocolla will enhance the innate spirituality of those born under the sign of Taurus.

Citrine: This stone's luminous yellow will warm the hearts of those born under the sign of Taurus. Citrine will drive away Taurus's anxiety and fear. This beautiful stone will also strengthen intellectual faculties and powers of concentration.

Emerald: The color of tender grass, the emerald is attractive to Taurus. Said to balance both the spirit and the body, the emerald is another stone that will nurture the innate spirituality of those born under this sign. This stone will give Taurus natives the chance to ruminate on their life experience; it will also fill them with hope for the future.

Lapis lazuli: When choosing a lapis lazuli stone, find one that sparkles with particles of golden pyrite. This stone looks like a piece of the starry night sky. It is solidified azure, symbolizing the tangible ideals that those born under the sign of Taurus can manifest when they develop the virtues of patience and perseverance.

Malachite: This is one of the stones dedicated to Saint Francis of Assisi. Earthy Taurus, with his love of the natural world, is in harmony with this stone. Also a stone of fertility, those born under this sign will find their creative potential greatly magnified when wearing a ring that includes a malachite stone.

Blue sapphire: This stone brings love of justice and a thirst for truth. It will encourage Taurus to look within and discover the subtle forces that affect his life. This knowledge can free those born under the sign of Taurus from self-defeating behavior.

Other good stones for those born under the sign of Taurus include: aventurine, azurite, beryl, chrysoberyl, coral, diamond, moldavite, obsidian, orpiment, rhodochrosite, rose quartz, and silicified wood.

GEMINI

May 21–June 21 • Element: Air • Ruling planet: Mercury

 Quick-witted, mercurial Geminis are born communicators. Ruled by the planet Mercury, Gemini natives are intellectual, curious, and literary. Those born under this sign are often drawn to the communications fields—newspapers, magazines, television, and radio.

Amber: This stone's static electricity is in harmony with the lively nature of Gemini. Amber will help those born under this sign to recharge their batteries when their energy runs low. This beautiful yellow stone also protects against bad moods.

Aquamarine: This stone, evoking the sea and its oceanic powers will add emotional depth to this sometimes shallow sign. A stone of prophets, shamans, and mystics, aquamarine will strengthen Gemini's intuitive abilities.

Celestine: This gentle stone will stimulate spiritual maturity in Gemini. It will also bring tranquility and balance. In addition, celestine will help those born under this sign to find more compatible romantic partners.

Chalcedony: Often called the "speaker's stone," chalcedony is tailor-made for Gemini, the most verbal sign in the zodiac. This stone will help those born under this sign to express themselves clearly, and "think on their feet." The blue variety is best for Gemini natives. But be careful: a tendency to stay "in the clouds" can be activated by chalcedony. It is best to add a complementary red stone.

Citrine: This stone's yellow clarity will help Gemini natives to sort out the tangled web of their desires and passions. Citrine will help them to better understand their sometimes contradictory feelings and needs.

Rock crystal: The nonrefracted light of this beautiful mineral is particularly compatible with the sign of Gemini. The stone of purity, rock crystal will bring tolerance, emotional strength, and clarity to this intellectual sign.

Tiger's eye: A look of a wild animal, an acuteness that's sometimes disquieting—this beautiful stone will help Gemini natives to see life more clearly. Moreover, the tiger's eye will increase their concentration and focus.

Topaz: Ruled by the planet Mercury, Gemini natives are great teachers. Yellow or golden topaz will help them to communicate their knowledge to others. It will also help them to focus, and guard against their tendency to be "a jack of all trades."

Other good stones for those born under the sign of Gemini include: moss agate, yellow carnelian, jet, obsidian, and pyrite.

CANCER

June 22–July 22 • Element: Water • Ruling planet: Moon

Often hypersensitive, Cancer is a nurturing, family-oriented sign. Cancer natives of both sexes have a domestic bent and feel most comfortable at home. Their warmth, charm, and culinary excellence make them exceptional hosts.

Aventurine: This stone will help to calm Cancer natives confronted with hectic schedules or surrounded by the hustle and bustle of big city living. Aventurine will also help them absorb the beneficial energies of the natural world.

Celestine: This stone will bring moody Cancer a feeling of tranquility and peace and can reduce depression. The power of its beautiful blue color will also help natives of this sign to open up spiritually.

Coral: With its marine roots, coral is a natural fit for watery Cancer. The color of this energizing red stone will help those born under this sign to feel stronger and more adventurous.

Emerald: This beautiful green stone was once used as a magnifying glass. The emerald will help Cancers to quiet their emotions and "see" things more clearly. This stone will also have an invigorating effect on their thinking process.

Jade: This stone, connected to motherhood, is in harmony with the nurturing sign of Cancer. In some cultures, jade is thought to ease the pain of childbirth, and laboring women are given a jade stone or figurine to hold in their hands. This stone offers Cancer a feeling of calm strength and serenity in the midst of an emotional storm.

Jasper: This is the "mothers'" stone, another symbol of motherhood and birth. This stone will connect Cancer natives with the primordial force of nature and fill them with compassion and patience.

Moonstone: This stone get its name from its beautiful, milky white color. A lunar stone, the moonstone will help men born under this sign get in touch with their feminine side. It is a stone of passion and eroticism. It can strengthen the intuition of Cancer natives, especially in regards to the destiny of their beloved.

Opal: This lunar stone is Cancer's favorite. The opal will put natives of this sign in touch with their feelings and help them to think carefully before acting.

Pearl: This sensual stone is called the "Divine Mother" in India. Another symbol of the feminine, the pearl will help Cancers of both sexes to rebound after an emotional trauma. It will allow them to transform their pain into something creative and hopeful.

Other good stones for those born under the sign of Cancer include: aragonite, beryl, calcite, red carnelian, chalcedony, chrysoberyl, jade, jet, labradorite, malachite, meerschaum, mica, moldavite, nephrite, rhodochrosite, scepter crystal, sulfur, and zirconium.

LEO

July 23–August 22 • Element: Fire • Ruling planet: Sun

 The most royal of the fire signs, Leo is proud, courageous, and ambitious. Leo natives naturally gravitate to positions of leadership and power. Ruled by the Sun, this sign likes to shine; Leos of both sexes have a distinctly regal bearing.

Amber: A veritable amplifier of solar force, amber is a perfect match for Leo. This stone will make it possible for Leos to balance their fiery nature with periods of quiet contemplation.

Citrine: The lemon yellow color of this stone is invigorating to those born under the sign of Leo. It will stimulate their creative faculties and encourage them to make their dreams a reality.

Diamond: The word *diamond* comes from the Greek *adamas,* meaning "untameable." Its grandeur makes it a perfect fit for the royal lion. A diamond will strengthen the vital energy of all Leo natives.

Garnet: Leos can make good use of the passionate energy of this stone. Garnet symbolizes the primordial fire, and this stone will help them purify their negative emotions.

Olivine: This beautiful stone can help Leos to open their hearts to others. It can also help heal cardiovascular problems. Olivine can inspire Leos to express themselves with eloquence and passion. It is also a beneficial stone for the entrepreneurs and artists of this sign.

Ruby: Leo will appreciate the deep red color of this beautiful stone. Garnet's "older brother," the ruby is an aphrodisiac, and this stone will help Leos to connect more deeply with their partners. But be careful; the ruby can also exacerbate natural aggressiveness.

Other good stones for those born under the sign of Leo include: amazonite, calcite, chrysolite, chrysoprase, rock crystal, orpiment, peridot, pyrite, rhodonite, and tiger's eye.

VIRGO

August 23–September 22 • Element: Earth • Ruling planet: Mercury

Level-headed but critical, Virgos have a mental orientation to life. Natural teachers, Virgo natives excel in academic and technical fields. This kind, gentle, and shy sign is often criticized for emphasizing the mind at the expense of their hearts.

Yellow agate: This yellow color warms the hearts of all Virgo natives. The yellow agate is also a stone of seduction; its beautiful warm glow will help them attract members of the opposite sex.

Carnelian: A beautiful orange carnelian will complete the action of the other stones by giving Virgo the satisfaction of a job well done. This stone will give Virgos a feeling of gratitude and joy. Carnelian can also heal sexual problems.

Citrine: This invigorating stone will give Virgos a healthy boost of confidence and optimism. This miniature sun is charged with solar energy that will encourage them to take action.

Red jasper: A stone that is gentle to the touch, red jasper has a stimulating effect on Virgo. This stone of determination will give Virgo natives the strength and persistence they need to achieve their goals.

Lapis lazuli: This beautiful blue "sky stone" will bring a sense of balance to earthy Virgo. Like the ancient Egyptians, Virgo natives can use a lapis lazuli stone as a good luck charm.

Yellow sapphire: This beautiful stone will make it easier for shy Virgos to express themselves verbally. It is also a good stone for meditation and contemplation.

Other good stones for those born under the sign of Virgo include: alabaster, amber, amethyst, ametrine, calcite, jet, orpiment, black pearl, silicified wood, sodalite, sulfur, sunstone, and tiger's eye.

LIBRA

September 23–October 22 • Element: Air • Ruling planet: Venus

 Can love be wise? Can you reason with Venus? Such is the paradox of the Venus ruled sign of Libra. In addition to their well-deserved reputation for romance and sensuality, Libras are known for their excellent taste in art. Peace-loving and gentle, natives of this sign aspire to a life of harmony and grace.

Aquamarine: A stone of prophets, shamans, and mystics, aquamarine evokes the watery depths of the sea. This beautiful blue stone will help Libras get in touch with their innate inner wisdom. Aquamarine also aids meditation.

Chrysocolla: The stone of peace, compassion, and forgiveness, chrysocolla is the perfect stone for gentle Libra. Its calming energy will also help to reduce the anxieties of first-time mothers.

Pink coral: This stone will help the peace loving Libra to be more assertive. Wearing a pink coral ring will give Libras the confidence to speak their mind and hold their ground.

Gem salt: Libras often shrink from the harsh realities of life. This mineral will help them face unpleasant truths and make difficult or painful decisions.

Orpiment: This brilliant yellow stone will boost Libras' self-confidence and fill them with the joy of living. Orpiment is the perfect remedy for sadness and depression.

Sapphire: This is another stone conducive to introspection. For those born under this sign, the sapphire will stimulate a spiritual search.

Smoky quartz: This stone symbolizes resurrection and rebirth. It can give gentle Libra the courage to look within and heal long buried wounds. Smoky quartz is also an aphrodisiac that will enhance the sensuality of this Venus ruled sign.

Topaz: Yellow or, better yet, golden topaz has a balancing effect on Libra. This stone will stabilize the Libra natives who often waver between head and heart.

Other good stones for those born under the sign of Libra include: alabaster, calcite, citrine, jade, kunzite, rose quartz, silicified wood, and pink tourmaline.

SCORPIO

October 23–November 21 • Element: Water • Ruling planet: Pluto

 The sign of evolution, change, and renewal, Scorpio is the most formidable sign in the zodiac. This powerful sign has an aggressive, confrontational nature that can frighten the more timid signs. A water sign, Scorpio is often associated with the occult, and many Scorpio natives have a deep and penetrating insight into the unseen worlds. Those born under this sign need stabilizing stones to balance their agitation and anger.

Agate: This stone enhances the inner life and aids meditation. Agate will help Scorpios to discover their inner light. But it cannot do everything; agates can point Scorpio in the right direction but determination and discipline are essential.

Garnet: This stone matches the intensity of Scorpio. It represents the primordial fire, the purification of love. Garnets will strengthen the resolve and perseverance of those born under this sign. But be careful: quick-tempered Scorpios should not remain in contact with this stone for more than 5 minutes a day.

Hematite: This stone will bring a bit of peace to Scorpio. Hematite drives out gloomy thoughts and makes people joyful. It will also encourage kindness and reduce the tendency to judge others.

Jet: Jet's calm vibration will help Scorpio natives to balance their volatile moods. Jet is also a good stone for meditation. Jet's black color is not gloomy; this is a powerful, protective stone.

Onyx: The earth's claw, the onyx will help Scorpio natives to feel rooted. This is another stone that will help to stabilize the volatile emotions of those born under this sign.

Ruby: Scorpio's sometimes hot temper will be calmed by this stone. However, be careful; in the beginning it can have the opposite effect. Rubies are also an aphrodisiac, and this stone can help Scorpios to deepen their relationships.

Other good stones for those born under the sign of Scorpio include: amazonite, andalusite, aragonite, aventurine, chrysolite, heliotrope, jasper, magnetite, malachite, obsidian, pearl, peridot, and black tourmaline.

SAGITTARIUS

November 22–December 20 • Element: Fire • Ruling planet: Jupiter

 In the ancient world, Sagittarius was considered the sign of the prophet. Modern day natives of this sign are known for their interest in religion and philosophy—the search for truth. One of the royal fire signs, Sagittarians are the aristocrats of the zodiac. Interested in the finer things of life, they are characterized by their refinement and generosity of spirit.

Amethyst: The gentle radiance of this stone will open the Sagittarius native's heart. Amethyst will also strengthen intuition and enhance creativity.

Aventurine: Green in color, this stone soothes the mind and gives hope for the future. Aventurine also helps Sagittarians appreciate and absorb the beneficial vibrations of the natural world.

Chrysocolla: This stone of peace and compassion is in tune with the generous nature of those born under this sign. Sagittarians should wear this stone when they need to forgive the careless behavior of someone close to them. This stone will also encourage Sagittarians to spend time in the home.

Lapis lazuli: A symbol of the starry night sky, this beautiful stone will expand Sagittarius's awareness of the greater, cosmic forces. Those born under this sign should meditate on this stone to strengthen their intuition and access to spiritual truths.

Obsidian: A stone of contrast, obsidian will help Sagittarians sort out the true from the false. This sacred stone will enable those born under this sign to get in touch with their deeper self and discover their true feelings and needs.

Opal: This is a stone of clarity and white light. The opal will strengthen Sagittarians' ability to see and understand the true motives of those around them. It will also aid memory and reduce depression.

Sapphire: One of the most harmonious stones for this sign, the sapphire is associated with a love of justice and a thirst for truth. Sagittarians should meditate on this stone when they need to make an important, life-changing decision.

Sodalite: This stone will help Sagittarians concentrate. It can also help them to be less dependent on other people's opinions.

Turquoise: The sky blue color of this stone is mixed with the luxuriant green of nature. As such, it has a balancing effect on those born under this sign. Turquoise will help Sagittarius to negotiate with tact and charm.

Other good stones for those born under the sign of Sagittarius include: ametrine, azurite, calcite, celestine, chalcedony, meerschaum, blue topaz, and zirconium.

CAPRICORN

December 21–January 19 • Element: Earth • Ruling planet: Saturn

 This practical earth sign values security, logic, and tradition. Capricorns are organized, disciplined, and conscientious. Natives of this sign are known for their ambition and business savvy; their perseverance eventually leads to success.

Amethyst: This beautiful stone is conducive to meditation and will strengthen Capricorns' intuition—always a plus in the fast paced world of business. Amethyst will help Capricorns achieve success.

Chalcedony: This is another stone that encourages reflection and meditation. Often called the "speaker's stone," chalcedony will help Capricorns choose their words carefully. Capricorns should carry a chalcedony in their pocket when they negotiate a business deal—or ask for a raise.

Diamond: Capricorns, with their taste for fundamentals, will feel at home with this stone. The diamond is the hardest stone, and the only mineral composed of a single element. This is the ideal stone for diligent contemplation and deep meditation. The diamond's light corresponds to the inner light found deep within each human being.

Emerald: The soft green color of early spring will connect Capricorn to the cycle of life. The emerald encourages meditation and reflection in this practical sign and helps correct a tendency toward intolerance. Emerald will also help Capricorns activate their latent creativity.

Jasper: There is something earthy and primordial in this stone that will appeal to Capricorn. Jasper radiates a calm that will help the often stubborn natives of this sign to have more compassion and patience with others.

Obsidian: This ambiguous stone has a special affinity with Capricorn. The obsidian will reveal the profound layers of Capricorn's being and put those born under this sign in touch with their deepest feelings and needs.

Pearl: The charm and seduction of this sensual stone has a welcoming aura that will aid Capricorns in love or in business. It will also help Capricorns express the softer emotions that they often keep bottled up inside.

Other good stones for those born under the sign of Capricorn include: ametrine, azurite, calcite, celestine, chalcedony, meerschaum, onyx, blue topaz, and zirconium.

AQUARIUS

January 20–February 18 • Element: Air • Ruling planet: Uranus

 Aquarius is the most progressive sign of the zodiac. Aquarius natives are future-oriented, independent, and unconventional. Many of the greatest innovators and inventors were born under this sign.

Aquamarine: This beautiful blue stone is connected to the sea. Aquamarine will help Aquarians explore the depths of their soul and discover their intuitive gifts.

Chrysocolla: This is another stone that can help navigate the twists and turns of life. Chrysocolla will calm anxiety, depression, and feelings of guilt. It will also make it easier for Aquarians to meet their obligations.

Fluorite: This "stone of the genius" has a particular affinity with the innovative sign of Aquarius. Its radiance is conducive to scientific research and information technology—fields where Aquarians shine. The blue variety especially inspires Aquarius's creativity.

Opal: This lunar stone will have a calming effect on those born under this sign. It reduces depression, and it will help Aquarians to stop brooding and focus their thoughts in a more positive direction.

Sapphire: This brilliant stone is especially attractive to future-oriented Aquarians. It will stimulate new ideas, and help them to make the creative "leaps" that are the hallmark of this sign.

Turquoise: This stone is a good-luck charm for people born under this sign. Turquoise will protect Aquarians from adversity and enable them to recognize both their true—and their false—friends. It strengthens the will and provides a spark of inspiration for the projects of Aquarius natives.

Other good stones for those born under the sign of Aquarius include: celestine, gem salt, tiger's eye (particularly falcon's eye), and topaz.

PISCES

February 19–March 20 • Element: Water • Ruling planet: Neptune

 Pisces, symbolized by two fish, is the most sensitive and intuitive sign of the zodiac. Those born under this sign are imaginative, compassionate, and kind. Profoundly idealistic, they often gravitate to the helping professions.

Amethyst: This stone, a symbol of spiritual purity, is a perfect fit for Pisces. The radiance of amethyst is conducive to meditation, and this stone will stimulate creativity, imagination, and intuition.

Andalusite: This stone will provide emotional balance for sensitive Pisces. Andalusite will help Pisceans enjoy nature and feel more anchored to Earth.

Coral: A marine mineral is another perfect stone for Pisces. Coral, which grows on the ocean floor, can provide a sense of stability for this watery sign.

Jade: In Asia, and pre-Columbian America, many jade amulets are found in the shape of a fish. This makes clear the affinity between Pisces and this mineral. Jade does not bring anything specific to those born under this sign. Even so, it will give a feeling of overall well-being and self-confidence.

Labradorite: This grayish stone only reveals its sparkling colors when it's examined closely. In the same way, people often overlook quiet, unassuming Pisces. Once we look beyond the surface, we see the sparkling qualities of those born under this sign. The radiance of this stone will make their virtues more readily apparent.

Olivine: This is also a protective stone for Pisces. In addition, it will help heal cardiovascular problems for those born under this sign. Do not wear an olivine with another stone: their vibrations will counteract one another.

Pearl: The silky brilliance of this stone will help Pisceans to weather the ups and downs of life.

Turquoise: This is a talisman and protective stone for those born under the sign of Pisces. It will strengthen their memory and help them avoid deceitful people. Gentle and idealistic, Pisces is easily fooled. Those born under this sign can be the prey of charlatans and religious organizations interested in profiting from their often naive generosity. Turquoise will also guard against hypersensitivity.

Other good stones for those born under the sign of Pisces include: alabaster, ametrine, aquamarine, aventurine, calcite, fluorite, iolite, jet, kunzite, mica, moonstone, nephrite, opal, and tanzanite.

PART THREE

Treatment for Specific Conditions

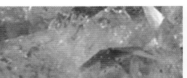

8

PHYSICAL CARE

Acne

Stones: Amazonite, andalusite, aventurine, garnet

Chakra: Anahata chakra (heart)

Colors: Green, pink

Instructions: Place the stone on the heart chakra for 20 minutes. Rinse the skin with amazonite water after washing it. Follow a balanced diet. Wear jewelry that includes a garnet.

Alcoholic Intoxication

Stones: Amethyst, tanzanite

Chakras: Sahasrara chakra (top of the head), Manipura chakra (solar plexus)

Colors: Yellow and its complementary color purple

Instructions: Wear jewelry that includes an amethyst as a preventative measure. If you attend a cocktail party, suck on an amethyst or a tanzanite for 5 minutes before, during, and after drinking alcohol. Keep an amethyst sewn into or under your pillow. Drink a lot of water.

Allergies (chronic or seasonal)

Stones: Aquamarine, amber, citrine

Chakra: Vishuddha chakra (throat)

Colors: Purple, and after the symptoms have diminished, yellow

Instructions: Massage the affected areas with aquamarine water mixed with one-third lemon juice. You can also drink aquamarine water. Wear jewelry with amber or citrine, or both. Place a fragment of amber on the throat chakra, and a piece of citrine on your forehead for 10 minutes.

Amenorrhea

See **Menstrual Disorders**

Anemia

Stones: Coral, heliotrope, hematite, jasper

Chakra: Svadhisthana chakra (sacrum)

Color: Orange

Instructions: Place the stone on the lower abdomen for 20 minutes. Mix coral powder in seasoning vinegar (a pinch for a teaspoon of vinegar). Drink a glass of heliotrope water three times a day. Wear a hematite jewel.

Angina

Stones: Azurite, chalcedony

Chakra: Vishuddha chakra (throat)

Colors: Light blue, blue-green

Instructions: Drink a teaspoon of azurite water morning and night for a week. Suck on a piece of chalcedony when you feel pain.

Arterial Tension

Stones: Beryl, chrysoberyl, chrysolite, chrysoprase, kunzite

Chakra: Anahata chakra (heart)

Colors: Green, pink, gold

Instructions: Drink a glass of beryl water three times a day. Place one of these stones on the heart area for 20 minutes.

Arthritis, Arthrosis

Stones: Meerschaum, garnet, malachite, sunstone

Chakra: According to the problem area

Colors: Orange, blue

Instructions: Massage the affected area with a piece of polished meerschaum. Alternate applying garnet and malachite on the corresponding chakra. For example, use malachite for 10 minutes in the morning and garnet for 10 minutes in the evening. Drink as much sunstone water as you want.

Bladder Problems

See **Kidney Illnesses or Incontinence**

Bloating

See **Digestive Disorders**

Buzzing in the Ears

Stone: Onyx

Chakra: Ajna chakra (brow)

Colors: Purple, black

Instructions: Don't wear an onyx constantly. Hold the stone or wear a jewel for 10 minutes at the most, several times a day.

Cardiac Problems

Stones: Agate, aventurine, emerald, garnet (unless there's hypertension), hematite (especially for arrhythmia), kunzite, lapis lazuli, moldavite, olivine (never use it with another stone)

Chakra: Anahata chakra (heart)

Color: Purple

Instructions: Place the stone on the heart chakra for 20 minutes. Wear an aventurine or hematite jewel on the skin in a pendant or ring. Drink emerald, lapis lazuli, or garnet water.

Chickenpox, Smallpox

Stone: Amazonite

Chakra: Anahata chakra (heart)

Color: Green, pink

Instructions: Place the stone on the heart chakra for 20 minutes as a complement to standard medical treatment.

See also Shingles

Childbirth, Pregnancy

Stones: Chrysocolla, coral, jade, moonstone

Chakra: Svadhisthana chakra (sacrum)

Color: Orange

Instructions: Place the stone on the lower abdomen for 20 minutes. Place a piece of jade in a pregnant woman's left hand.

Constipation

Stones: Diamond, topaz, peridot

Chakra: Svadhisthana chakra (sacrum)

Color: Orange

Instructions: Suck on a diamond, topaz, or peridot stone. Drink as much diamond or topaz water as you want, or drink half a glass of peridot water after each meal. Place diamond or topaz on the abdomen for 5 minutes only.

　　See also Digestive Disorders

Convalescence

See Fatigue

Diabetes

Stone: Citrine

Chakra: Svadhisthana chakra (sacrum)

Color: Orange

Instructions: Drink as much citrine water as you want to complement the standard medical treatment.

Diarrhea

Stones: Rock crystal, diamond

Chakra: Svadhisthana chakra (sacrum)

Color: Orange

Instructions: Suck on rock crystal. Place a diamond on the abdomen for 5 minutes only.

Digestive Disorders

Stones: Meerschaum, emerald, heliotrope, jasper, moldavite (for flatulence), opal (especially "fire opal")

Chakras: Manipura chakra (solar plexus), Svadhisthana chakra (sacrum)

Colors: Yellow gold, orange

Instructions: Place the stone on the area to be treated for several minutes, and then massage the chakra with your thumb in small circular movements for 3 minutes. You can also roll a little ball of meerschaum over the painful area. Drink as much emerald or heliotrope water as you want.

Eczema

Stones: Aventurine, jade

Chakra: Anahata chakra (heart)

Colors: Green, pink

Instructions: Place the stone on the heart chakra for 20 minutes, morning and evening. Eat lightly for two days and drink as much aventurine or jade water as you want.

Endocrine Gland Problems

Stones: Citrine, lapis lazuli

Chakra: Svadhisthana chakra (sacrum)

Color: Orange

Instructions: Drink as much citrine water as you want. Place a citrine on your lower abdomen for 20 minutes.

Epilepsy

Stone: Aquamarine, diamond

Chakras: Ajna chakra (brow), Sahasrara chakra (top of the head), Muladhara chakra (base of the spine)

Colors: Red, purple, blue

Instructions: In the morning, massage your temples with aquamarine water. After lunch, hold an aquamarine against your brow chakra for 20 minutes. In the early evening, sit relaxed with your back straight and place an aquamarine on the top of your head. Keep the stone there for 5 minutes. Last of all drink a glass of aquamarine water before going to bed. For treatment with a diamond, place the stone between your eyes for 5 minutes, three times a day.

Eye Disorders

Stones: Beryl, chrysoberyl, aquamarine, emerald, lapis lazuli, moldavite

Chakras: Anahata chakra (heart), Ajna chakra (brow)

Colors: Blue-green, purple, pink, gold

Instructions: Drink one glass of beryl water, three times a day. Place one of these stones on the heart chakra. Close your eyes and put an aquamarine or lapis lazuli stone on your eyelids for 20 minutes before going to bed.

Eye Strain or Fatigue

Stones: Aquamarine, herkimer crystal, rock crystal, moldavite

Chakra: Ajna chakra (brow)

Colors: Blue, purple

Instructions: Close your eyes and put an aquamarine or a moldavite stone on your eyelids for 20 minutes before going to bed. Drink as much crystal water as you like.

Fatigue, Weakness, Convalescence

Stones: Silicified Wood, chalcedony

Chakra: Sahasrara chakra (top of the head)

Colors: Purple, gold

Instructions: Sit up straight and balance the stone on the top of your head for 2 or 3 minutes.

Fever

Stones: Agate, gem salt, sulfur

Chakra: Ajna chakra (brow)

Colors: Purple, blue

Instructions: Hold one of these stones against your forehead. Drink a glass of agate water three times a day. Apply several salt crystals to the chest or forehead. Let them melt by means of perspiration. Massage your temples with a sulfur stone.

Flatulence

See **Digestive Disorders**

Flu

Stone: Jade
Chakras: Anahata chakra (heart), Vishuddha chakra (throat)
Colors: Light blue, green
Instructions: Suck on this stone and hold it against the chakras.

Frigidity

See **Sexual Problems**

Gallbladder

Stone: Chrysolite
Chakra: Svadhisthana chakra (sacrum)
Color: Orange
Instructions: Place the stone on the lower abdomen for 15 minutes, morning and night.

Gastric Acidity

See **Digestive Disorders**

Hay Fever

See **Allergies**

Headaches

See **Migraine Headaches**

Hemorrhoids

Stones: Garnet, heliotrope, jasper

Chakras: Muladhara chakra (base of the spine), Svadhisthana chakra (sacrum)

Colors: Red, orange

Instructions: Suck on a garnet. Place a garnet or heliotrope stone on your lower abdomen. Take a sitz bath in heliotrope water. Place jasper on the chakras at your lower abdomen and at the base of your spine.

Hives

Stones: Aventurine, aquamarine

Chakra: Anahata chakra (heart)

Colors: Green, pink

Instructions: Place the stone on your heart chakra for 20 minutes, morning and night. Eat lightly for two days. Drink as much aventurine water as you like. Rinse the irritated areas in aquamarine water. If the problems come from food poisoning (seafood, etc.), see the Allergies entry to complete the treatment.

Hoarseness

Stones: Azurite, chalcedony

Chakra: Vishuddha chakra (throat)

Colors: Light blue, blue green

Instructions: Drink a teaspoon of azurite water morning and evening for one week. Suck on a piece of chalcedony if your throat is sore.

Impotence

See **Sexual Problems**

Incontinence

Stones: Nephrite, zirconium

Chakra: Svadhisthana chakra (sacrum)

Color: Orange

Instructions: Suck on a stone before going to bed.

Insomnia

Stone: Amethyst

Chakra: Ajna chakra (brow)

Color: Purple

Instructions: Hold the stone to your forehead, between the eyes, for 20 minutes.

Kidney Illnesses

Stones: Chrysoprase, chrysolite, diamond, jasper

Chakra: Svadhisthana chakra (sacrum)

Colors: Orange, white

Instructions: Place the stone for 20 minutes on the kidneys or the bladder area or lower on the abdomen, at the Svadhisthana chakra.

Lumbago

See Rheumatism

Lung Disorders

See Respiratory Problems

Menstrual Disorders

Stones: Chrysocolla, coral, jet, lapis lazuli, magnetite, malachite, ruby, moonstone

Chakra: Svadhisthana chakra (sacrum)

Color: Orange

Instructions: Place the stone on the painful area. For lack of menstruation or abnormal discharge, place a stone on your lower abdomen for 20 minutes. Mix coral powder with vinegar (a pinch for a teaspoon of vinegar).

See also Migraine Headaches

Migraine Headaches

Stones: Amethyst, jade, tanzanite

Chakra: Ajna chakra (brow)

Color: Purple

Instructions: Hold an amethyst or jade stone between your eyes for 20 minutes.

Motion Sickness

Stones: Rock crystal, tourmaline

Chakra: Svadhisthana chakra (sacrum)

Color: Orange

Instructions: Suck on a rock crystal. Prick the heart area with a short tourmaline stick.

Nervous Disorders

Stones: Chrysocolla, diamond

Chakra: Ajna chakra (brow)

Color: Blue

Instructions: Place the stone between your eyes for 20 minutes. After there has been an improvement, yellow, and then purple colors can be beneficial.

Nosebleeds

Stones: Garnet, heliotrope, hematite, jade, jasper, topaz, sapphire

Chakra: Ajna chakra (brow)

Color: Orange

Instructions: Hold a stone against your forehead for 20 minutes.

Obesity

Stone: Magnesite

Chakra: Manipura chakra (solar plexus)

Colors: Yellow, golden yellow, orangey yellow

Instructions: Place the stone on the solar plexus chakra.

Pain

Stones: Herkimer crystal, magnetite

Chakra: According to the location of the pain

Colors: Translucent white, light blue

Instructions: Place on the painful place or on the closest chakra. If the pain is located between two chakras, alternate. You can also aim at the painful area with the tip of a Herkimer crystal. Use a bandage made of natural fibers to keep a piece of magnetite on the painful spot.

Parkinson's Disease

Stones: Rhodonite, rhodochrosite

Chakra: Ajna chakra (brow)

Colors: Blue, purple

Instructions: Drink one glass a day of rhodochrosite water for two weeks. Then drink a glass a day of rhodonite water for three weeks. This remedy can only complement the standard medical treatments.

Pregnancy

See Childbirth

Priapism (persistent erection of the penis, often painful, and without sexual excitement)

See Sexual Problems

Respiratory Problems

Stones: Aquamarine, pyrite, sapphire, turquoise

Chakras: Anahata chakra (heart), Vishuddha chakra (throat), Manipura chakra (solar plexus)

Colors: Purple, green, pink

Instructions: Massage the chest with aquamarine, sapphire, or turquoise water. If there is pain, massage the chest with one of these stones. Use a bandage made of natural fibers to keep a piece of pyrite on the chest and leave it there for an hour. Add gold if nausea accompanies shortness of breath.

Rheumatism, Lumbago

Stones: Garnet, jet, amber, lapis lazuli (for lumbago), malachite

Chakras: According to location

Colors: Red, green

Instructions: Place the stone on the corresponding chakras. The combination of amber and jet is very effective. You can "electrify" these stones by rubbing them on a wool cloth before applying them to the painful areas.

Sexual Problems

Stones: Amazonite, garnet, amethyst, amber, jasper, tourmaline (for impotence, frigidity); ruby, pyrite, quartz, and sunstone (as aphrodisiacs); zirconium

Chakras: Muladhara chakra (base of spine), Svadhisthana chakra (sacrum)

Colors: Red, orange

Instructions: Place a stone on the chakras. Massage the genital organs with amazonite or garnet water, morning, noon, and night. Place a garnet on the navel three times a day for 10 minutes. Place a tourmaline, amethyst, or ruby on the navel for 20 minutes in the morning and at night. Keep an amethyst sewn into your pillow or under it. Grate amber with a nutmeg grater and drink 1 or 2 pinches of the powder in a glass of water. Drink one-third of the glass, morning, noon, and night.

Shingles

Stones: Aquamarine, rhodochrosite

Chakra: Manipura chakra (solar plexus)

Colors: Yellow, gold

Instructions: Never put these stones in contact with the lesions. Place the stones on the chakra for 20 minutes, morning and night. This treatment will serve as a complement to the standard treatments.

See also Chickenpox

Smallpox

See Chickenpox

Stomach and Liver Problems

Stones: Aquamarine, jet

Chakra: Manipura chakra (solar plexus)

Colors: Yellow, gold

Instructions: Place a stone on the painful place for 5 minutes, three times a day. At night, before going to bed, place the stone on the chakra for about 20 minutes.

Suprarenal Glands Problems

Stone: Aventurine

Chakra: Svadhisthana chakra (sacrum)

Color: Orange

Instructions: Place the stone on the lower abdomen for 20 minutes, morning and night. Drink aventurine water.

Toothache
Stones: Aquamarine, amber (especially for teething pains in infants)
Chakra: Vishuddha chakra (throat)
Color: Purple
Instructions: Suck on a small aquamarine as you would on a piece of candy. Make a mouthwash with aquamarine water and add three drops of essence of anise per glass. For an infant's teething pains, sew a fragment of amber in the child's clothes. Rub his gums with a pinch of saffron in amber water.

Urinary Problems
See **Kidney Illnesses**

Vaginitis
See **Sexual Problems**

Varicose Veins
Stones: Garnet, heliotrope
Chakras: Muladhara chakra (base of the spine), Svadhisthana chakra (sacrum)
Colors: Red, orange
Instructions: Pour garnet water over the blocked veins. Suck on a piece of garnet. Place a garnet or heliotrope stone on your lower abdomen (at the Svadhisthana chakra).

Voice Disorders
Stones: Chalcedony

Chakra: Vishuddha chakra (throat)

Colors: Light blue, silver

Instructions: Place the stone on the area to be treated for several minutes. Drink a glass of chalcedony water three times a day. You can also suck on a small chalcedony stone.

Whooping Cough

Stone: Aquamarine

Chakra: Vishuddha chakra (throat)

Color: Purple

Instructions: Place the stone on your throat for 20 minutes. This therapy accelerates and complements the standard medical treatment.

9
PSYCHOLOGICAL CARE

Agitation, Destructive Aggressiveness

Stones: Aventurine, fluorine

Chakra: Anahata chakra (heart)

Colors: Green, pink, gold

Instructions: Place one of these stones on the heart chakra for 20 minutes, three times a day. Drink aventurine water. This treatment is especially suitable for teenagers.

Aggressiveness, Irrational Anger

Stones: Amethyst, aragonite, olivine, orpiment, pearl

Chakra: Anahata chakra (heart)

Colors: Green, pink, gold

Instructions: Place one of these stones on the heart chakra for 20 minutes, three times a day. Olivine should be used alone. Dissolve aragonite or a dead pearl in vinegar and use as a seasoning in food.

Alcoholism

Stones: Amethyst, tanzanite

Chakras: Muladhara chakra (base of the spine), Ajna chakra (brow)

Color: Red, blue, silver

Instructions: Place a stone in the bottom of your drinking glass. Wear a ring ornamented with an amethyst. Place the amethyst on the Muladhara chakra at the base of the spine and the tanzanite on the Ajna chakra, between the eyes for 20 minutes in the morning. Switch the stones' positions and repeat at night before going to bed.

Anorexia

Stones: Silicified wood, chalcedony, coral, jade

Chakra: Manipura chakra (solar plexus)

Colors: Yellow, gold, brown

Instructions: Place one of these stones on the chakra for 20 minutes, three times a day. Vinegar or lemon juice mixed with coral powder can be used as a seasoning for food. Wear a jade ring directly against the skin.

Anxiety

Stones: Chrysocolla, magnetite, peridot

Chakra: Anahata chakra (heart)

Colors: Gold, green, pink

Instructions: Tape a stone to each temple with a bandage made of natural fibers.

Bulimia

Stones: Magnetite, amber, chalcedony, coral

Chakra: Manipura chakra (solar plexus)

Colors: Yellow, gold, brown

Instructions: Place the stones on this chakra in rotation for 20 minutes, three times a day. Wear a ring mixing magnetite and amber or chalcedony. Use vinegar containing coral powder as a seasoning for food.

Concentration Difficulties

Stones: Amethyst, beryl (especially heliodore), chalcedony, chrysoberyl, chrysoprase, fluorite

Chakra: Ajna chakra (brow)

Colors: Blue, purple

Instructions: Place the chosen stone (let yourself go with your aesthetic preference) on the chakra, between the eyes. In certain cases (distraction, for example), add a red-colored stone, such as garnet or orpiment, to a chalcedony. Chrysoberyl is especially suitable for people born under the sign of Cancer.

Conformity or Pathological Normality

Stones: Jade, jasper, sodalite

Chakras: Anahata chakra (heart), Ajna chakra (brow), Sahasrara chakra (top of the head)

Colors: Red, blue

Instructions: Rotate the chosen stone to each of the chakras for 20 minutes. This disorder can cause us to become a slave to fashion—or even to join a cult.

Coprolalia (obsessive or uncontrollable use of obscene language; a symptom of Tourette's syndrome)

Stones: Amber, amethyst, coral

Chakra: Svadhisthana chakra (sacrum)

Color: Orange

Instructions: Drink amber water and use a pinch of amber powder mixed with food. Place the amethyst on the lower abdomen for 20 minutes, morning and night.

Depression

Stones: Yellow or crimson agate, amber, chalcedony, chrysocolla, coral, lapis lazuli, obsidian, opal, peridot, aragonite, pearl, quartz (except rose)

Chakra: Ajna chakra (brow)

Colors: Yellow, purple

Instructions: Wear an agate stone directly against the skin. Warning: agate can initially worsen symptoms. Drink three glasses a day of chalcedony, lapis lazuli, opal, or chrysocolla water. Use vinegar containing coral powder, or vinegar in which you have dissolved aragonite or a dead pearl, as a seasoning for food. The obsidian/rock crystal combination applied to the Ajna chakra for 20 minutes is the supreme remedy.

Disappointments in Love

Stones: Amazonite, garnet

Chakras: Anahata chakra (heart), Ajna chakra (brow), Sahasrara chakra (top of the head)

Colors: Red, blue

Instructions: Rotate the chosen stone to each of the chakras for 20 minutes.

Domestic Disputes

Stones: Aventurine, amethyst, orpiment

Chakras: Ajna chakra (brow), Anahata chakra (heart), Muladhara chakra (base of the spine)

Colors: Purple, gold

Instructions: When calm, each person should place the stones on their partner's chakras.

Emotional Blockages

Stones: Amazonite, rhodochrosite, sunstone, moonstone, sapphire, tourmaline

Chakra: Svadhisthana chakra (sacrum)

Color: Orange

Instructions: Place one of the stones on the chakra at your lower abdomen for 20 minutes.

Envy

See Jealousy

Frigidity

Stones: Alabaster

Chakra: Svadhisthana chakra (sacrum)

Color: Orange

Instructions: Drink one glass of alabaster water three times a day. Also see the remedies for Impotence.

Guilt Feelings

Stones: Chrysocolla, jade, labradorite, sodalite

Chakra: Anahata chakra (heart)

Colors: Blue, purple

Instructions: Place one of these stones on the heart chakra for 20 minutes.

Hyperactivity, Nervous Energy

Stones: Agate, aquamarine

Chakras: Ajna chakra (brow)

Color: Purple

Instructions: Drink as much agate water as you like. Wear an aquamarine jewel.

Hysteria

Stones: Emerald, amethyst, orpiment

Chakras: Ajna chakra (brow), Muladhara chakra (base of the spine), Svadhisthana chakra (sacrum)

Colors: Blue, yellow

Instructions: Drink emerald water as a complement to an in-depth treatment. Rotate the stones to each of the chakras for 20 minutes during intense episodes.

Impotence

Stones: Amazonite, rhodochrosite, sunstone, moonstone, sapphire, tourmaline

Chakra: Svadhisthana chakra (sacrum)

Color: Orange

Instructions: Place the stone on the lower abdomen or genitals for 20 minutes.

Insomnia

Stones: Hematite, sulfur

Chakras: Ajna chakra (brow), Anahata chakra (heart), Muladhara chakra (base of the spine)

Colors: Blue, yellow, pink, red

Instructions: Rotate the stones to each of the chakras. Insomnia is a manifestation of stress, anxiety, and depression. Refer to these entries. Morning insomnia is specific to depressive conditions. It is sometimes accompanied by hyperactivity, which conceals the symptoms. In this case, more in-depth treatment will be needed.

Jealousy and Obsessive Envy

Stones: Chrysocolla, citrine, diamond, rhodonite

Chakras: Manipura chakra (solar plexus), Ajna chakra (brow)

Colors: Yellow, blue, indigo

Instructions: Use these stones as a complement to in-depth psychiatric treatment. Place a stone on the chosen chakra for 20 minutes. Do not use citrine if you have a violent temperament or a tendency toward slander.

Low Libido (without physical disorders)

Stones: Amazonite, jasper, zirconium, tourmaline

Chakra: Svadhisthana chakra (sacrum)

Color: Orange

Instructions: Suck on the stone and place it on your lower abdomen for 20 minutes.

Memory Problems

Stones: Emerald, fluorine, malachite, moldavite, opal

Chakra: Ajna chakra (brow)

Colors: Blue, yellow

Instructions: Memory problems without lesions in the nerve centers often have an emotional basis. In-depth treatment will be necessary. Drinking as much as you like of emerald and malachite water will help to cure this problem more quickly. You should also place a fluorine, opal, or moldavite stone between your eyes for 20 minutes, three times a day.

Mental Degeneration

Stones: Moldavite, mica, nephrite

Chakras: Ajna chakra (brow), Manipura chakra (solar plexus)

Colors: Yellow, purple, gold

Instructions: Place a stone on one of the chakras for 20 minutes.

Moroseness, Pessimism, Defeatism

Stones: Chalcedony, fluorine, jade, jet

Chakra: Ajna chakra (brow)

Colors: Yellow, purple, gold

Instructions: Drink a glass of chalcedony water, three times a day. Place the fluorine stone between the eyes for 20 minutes. Wear a jade ring that touches the skin. Also wear a jet jewel such as a brooch. Be careful: contact with the skin tarnishes jet.

Nightmares

Stones: Hematite, chrysocolla, jade, moonstone, sunstone

Chakras: Ajna chakra (brow), Sahasrara chakra (top of the head)

Colors: Red, blue

Instructions: Place these stones in the bedroom.

See also Anxiety; Depression

Nymphomania

See Sexual Obsession

Paranoia

See Personality Alterations

Personality Alterations

Stones: Alabaster, fluorine, moldavite, obsidian, tanzanite

Chakras: Muladhara chakra (base of the spine), Ajna chakra (brow)

Colors: Red, purple

Instructions: In cases of sluggishness place one of these stones under your pillow. For other problems, drink a quart of water with one teaspoon of alabaster powder during the day for one week. Place a fluorine stone between your eyes for 20 minutes. Put a moldavite, tanzanite, or obsidian stone under your pillow or sew into your nightclothes. All stone treatments only aid in-depth, long-term, psychiatric treatment.

Pessimism

See **Moroseness, or Pessimism entry in chapter 10**

Postpartum Depression

See **Depression**

Selfishness

Stones: Aragonite, pearl

Chakra: Ajna chakra (brow)

Color: Blue

Instructions: Dissolve aragonite or a dead pearl in vinegar and use it as a seasoning for food.

Sexual Obsession or Addiction

Stones: Amazonite, amber, jasper, kunzite, sunstone, sapphire

Chakra: Svadhisthana chakra (sacrum)

Color: Orange

Instructions: Drink as much amazonite, sapphire, or amber water as you like. Add a pinch of amber powder to your food. Place jasper or sunstone on the lower abdomen for 20 minutes, three times a day. Kunzite, applied to the chakra in the same way, can also be beneficial. But use with precaution: it can cause us to lose touch with reality.

Shyness, Stage Fright

Stones: Chalcedony, mica, gem salt, turquoise

Chakras: Ajna chakra (brow), Manipura chakra (solar plexus)

Colors: Yellow, purple, gold

Instructions: Meditate with the stones. Alternate drinking one glass of chalcedony water three times a day and one glass of mica water three times a day. Place a turquoise or salt stone on the chakras.

Sleepwalking
Stone: Chalcedony
Chakra: Ajna chakra (brow)
Color: Yellow
Instructions: Sew a stone in the hem of your nightclothes.

Stress, Nervous Tension
Stones: Amethyst, jasper, tanzanite
Chakras: Ajna chakra (brow), Manipura chakra (solar plexus)
Colors: Yellow, purple, gold
Instructions: Place the stones on the chakras above for 20 minutes.

Tourette's Syndrome
Stones: Aventurine, amethyst, chrysocolla, chrysolite
Chakra: Ajna chakra (brow)
Colors: Blue, purple
Instructions: Place one of the stones at the chakra between your eyes twice a day for 20 minutes. This will help to reduce a crisis, but it should only be used as an aid to the standard medical treatment.

10

SPIRITUAL CARE

Balancing the Energetic Body

Stones: Emerald, amethyst, orpiment

Chakras: Ajna chakra (brow), Muladhara chakra (base of the spine), and Svadhisthana chakra (sacrum)

Colors: Blue, yellow

Instructions: Meditate on these stones.

Becoming More Caring

Stones: Aventurine, amethyst, orpiment

Chakras: Ajna chakra (brow), Muladhara chakra (base of the spine), Svadhisthana chakra (sacrum)

Colors: Blue, purple, gold

Instructions: Meditate on the chakras—feel them, think about them, and visualize them.

See also Inner Harmony

Brooding

See Depression in chapter 9. This is a form of spiritual masochism. We take pleasure in digging into the darkness of our souls. We may brood over previous depressions, obsessions, or anxieties.

Clarity

Stones: Amber, chalcedony, coral

Chakras: Muladhara chakra (base of the spine), Manipura chakra (solar plexus), Sahasrara chakra (top of the head)

Colors: Yellow, gold, red, purple, black

Instructions: Contemplate, and then meditate on your preferred stone. Reflect on the colors. Buzzing (mouth closed) on the sound *om,* gradually quiet your mind.

Communion with Nature

Stones: Aventurine, fluorine

Chakra: Anahata chakra (heart)

Colors: Green, pink, gold

Instructions: Meditate, and then chant the sound *yam* on the fourth note of the scale (F).

Communion with the Profound Self

Stones: Amazonite, amber, jasper, kunzite, sapphire, sunstone

Chakra: Svadhisthana chakra (sacrum)

Color: Orange

Instructions: Drink as much amazonite, amber, or sapphire water as you like. Place jasper, sapphire, or sunstone on the chakra for 20 minutes, three times a day. The kunzite applied in the same way will bring us back to autonomous spiritual altitude.

Concentration Problems

Stones: Amethyst, beryl (especially heliodore), chalcedony, chryso-beryl, chrysoprase, fluorite

Chakra: Ajna chakra (brow)

Colors: Blue, purple

Instructions: Choose the stone that appeals to you aesthetically and place it on the chakra between your eyes. In cases of distraction, use the chalcedony with a red-colored stone such as garnet or orpiment. Chrysoberyl is especially suited to people born under the sign of Cancer. These treatment options are particularly helpful for improving concentration during meditation.

Confidence in and Respect for the Forces of the Universe

Stones: Amethyst, tanzanite

Chakras: Muladhara chakra (base of the spine), Ajna chakra (brow)

Colors: Red, blue, silvery

Instructions: Meditate and let the amethyst's gentle vibrations—or the "spikier" vibrations of tanzanite—come into you. Murmur the sound *lam* from your throat.

Connection with the Forces of Natural Healing

Stones: Aventurine, fluorine

Chakra: Anahata chakra (heart)

Colors: Green, pink, gold

Instructions: Meditate and chant the sound *yam* on the fourth note of the scale (F).

Connection with the Terrestrial Forces

Stones: Amethyst, aragonite, olivine, orpiment, pearl

Chakra: Anahata chakra (heart)

Colors: Green, pink, gold

Instructions: Place one of the stones on the heart chakra for 20 minutes. Lay down and meditate. Repeat the sound *yam* in a series of seven without any particular tonality.

Depletion, Feelings of Emptiness

See Balancing the Energetic Body

Dialogue with the Higher Self

Stones: Agate, aquamarine

Chakra: Ajna chakra (brow)

Color: Purple

Instructions: Drink as much agate water as you want. Wear an aquamarine jewel. Chant the *aum* sound (with two syllables). Meditate on the color purple. Take a "silence bath" in a quiet place for 15 minutes every day. If this is impossible, use earplugs. The quiet will help you to hear your inner voice.

Energizing the Vital Force

Stones: Coral, chalcedony, fluorine, jade, jet

Chakra: Ajna chakra (brow)

Colors: Yellow, purple, gold, black

Instructions: Contemplate on the structure of the coral. Meditate on the blackness of the jet. Alternate placing fluorine and jade on the chakra between the eyes morning and night for 20 minutes. Spend 15 minutes in a silent place every day. If this is impossible, use earplugs. The quiet will help you to hear your inner voice.

Energy Blockage

Stones: Jade, jasper, sodalite, rock crystal, aquamarine

Chakras: Anahata chakra (heart), Ajna chakra (brow), Sahasrara chakra (top of the head)

Colors: Red, blue

Instructions: Rotate the stones on the chakras above for 20 minutes, five times a day.

Envy
See Jealousy

Excessive Materialism
Stones: Amazonite, alabaster

Chakra: Svadhisthana chakra (sacrum)

Color: Orange

Instructions: Drink one glass of alabaster water, three times a day. See also the Impotence and Frigidity remedies in chapter 9, as this is a type of spiritual impotence or frigidity. Lack of spiritual desire can also come from a psychological or preexisting physical disorder. Hum the sound *vam* on the second note of the scale (D).

False Spirituality
Stones: Rock crystal, aquamarine; serious cases: diamond

Chakra: Muladhara chakra (base of the spine)

Color: Translucent red

Instructions: An impression of spirituality or mystical loftiness hiding an artificial pride—often due to a feeling of inferiority. Chant the *lam* sound until you are out of breath. Empty your lungs and your mind. Place one of the stones on your heart. Meditate on the root chakra, an elementary force, which is simple and regenerative for the personality. It will make it possible to have a more down-to-earth vision of yourself and the world, which will restore your spiritual receptiveness—and mental health!

Feeling Ungrounded, Distracted

Stones: Silicified wood, chalcedony, coral, jade

Chakra: Manipura chakra (solar plexus)

Colors: Yellow, gold, brown

Instructions: Place the silicified wood on the solar plexus chakra for 20 minutes, three times a day. Hold the chalcedony gently and chant the sound *ram* on all the notes. Wear a jade jewel against your bare skin. Meditate on coral.

Greed, Preventing Spiritual Evolution

Stones: Amazonite, garnet

Chakras: Anahata chakra (heart), Ajna chakra (brow), Sahasrara chakra (top of the head)

Colors: Red, blue

Instructions: Place a stone on each of the chakras in rotation for 20 minutes.

Harnessing the Mental and Spiritual Forces

Stones: Hematite, sulfur

Chakra: Ajna chakra (brow), Anahata chakra (heart), Muladhara chakra (base of the spine)

Colors: Blue, yellow, green, pink, red

Instructions: Rotate the stones on the above chakras. Relax. Meditate on the colors and let the vibrations of the minerals wash over you.

Hatred

See Jealousy

Inner Harmony

Stones: Aventurine, amethyst, orpiment

Chakras: Ajna chakra (brow), Muladhara chakra (base of the spine), Svadhisthana chakra (sacrum)

Colors: Blue, purple, gold

Instructions: Rotate the stones to each of the chakras. Meditate and chant the sounds *om* (one syllable on the sixth note, A), *aum* (two syllables on the seventh note, B), *lam* (on the first note, C), and *vam* (on the second note, D).

Intolerance and Sectarianism

Stones: Jade, jasper, sodalite, rock crystal, aquamarine

Chakras: Anahata chakra (heart), Ajna chakra (brow), Sahasrara chakra (top of the head)

Colors: Red, blue

Instructions: No true spiritual search can be undertaken if we feel intolerant of others. Rotate the chosen stone on the chakras above for 20 minutes.

Intuitive Knowledge

Stones: Amber, amethyst, coral

Chakras: Ajna chakra (brow), Svadhisthana chakra (sacrum)

Color: Orange

Instructions: Meditate on the stones and the colors. Place an amber stone between your eyes for 20 minutes once a day. You may experience a period of insomnia following this treatment.

Jealousy, Envy, Hatred

Stones: Amazonite, garnet

Chakras: Anahata chakra (heart), Ajna chakra (brow), Sahasrara chakra (top of the head)

Colors: Red, blue

Instructions: These negative feelings block our spiritual progress. Rotate the chosen stone to each of the chakras for 20 minutes.

Knowledge of the Profound Self

Stones: Alabaster, fluorine, moldavite, obsidian, tanzanite

Chakras: Muladhara chakra (base of the spine), Ajna chakra (brow)

Colors: Red, purple

Instructions: Choose the stone that most attracts you. Alternate with the one you like the least. Try to analyze the reasons for this attraction and repulsion. Then, meditate on a stone of your choice in half—but not total—darkness. The sound *lam* should be hummed on the first note of the scale (C). Follow with the sound *om* or *aum* (with two syllables) in a deep voice until there's no breath left.

Memory

Stones: Emerald, fluorine, malachite, moldavite, opal

Chakra: Ajna chakra (brow)

Colors: Blue, yellow

Instructions: Ordinary memory is the psychic support of spiritual memory. The memory that goes beyond our own existence is necessary for all elevation. It will be restored with the healing of mental and emotional memory. Meditate on the stones and the colors. Chant the sound *aum* (with two syllables).

Pessimism, Defeatism

Stones: Chalcedony, fluorine, jade, jet

Chakra: Ajna chakra (brow)

Colors: Yellow, purple, gold, black

Instructions: Meditate. Place the fluorine on your forehead, between the eyes, for 20 minutes. Wear a jade jewel directly on the skin. Also wear a jet pin or broach. Spend 15 minutes every day in a quiet place. If this is impossible, use earplugs. The silence will allow you to hear your inner voice.

Proselytism (the need to convince or convert)
See Intolerance

Psychic Terror
Stones: Chalcedony, mica, gem salt, turquoise

Chakra: Ajna chakra (brow), Manipura chakra (solar plexus)

Colors: Yellow, purple, gold

Instructions: This condition can be brought about by too much mystical and spiritual concentration. Symptoms can include frightening hallucinations. Meditate and place a turquoise or salt stone on the chakras above. Avoid too much silence and solitude for several months.

Purifying Your Vital Energy to Connect with Mother Earth
Stones: Amazonite, jasper, zirconium, tourmaline

Chakra: Svadhisthana chakra (sacrum)

Color: Orange

Instructions: Place an amazonite on your lower abdomen for 20 minutes. Let your spirit feel free. The next day, meditate on a jasper stone while saying *vam* on the second note of the scale (D). The zirconium and the tourmaline can be used in active meditations as soon as you feel in direct contact with Mother Earth.

Reenergizing
Stones: Hematite, chrysocolla, jade, moonstone, sunstone

Chakras: Ajna chakra (brow), Sahasrara chakra (top of the head)

Colors: Red, blue

Instructions: First you must heal any possible depression. Then, place the hematite on the chakra between your eyes for 20 minutes in the morning. Place the chrysocolla or jade on the top of the head in the middle of the day for 20 minutes. Meditate on the colors and wear a moonstone or sunstone jewel. Hum the sound *om* from time to time without any particular intention, with detachment.

Sectarianism

See Intolerance

Spiritual Doubt

Stones: Chrysocolla, magnetite, peridot

Chakra: Anahata chakra (heart)

Color: Gold, green, pink

Instructions: Hold the stones gently while chanting the sound *lam* on all the notes.

Spiritual Indecision

Stone: Garnet

Chakra: Ajna chakra (brow)

Colors: Yellow, red

Instructions: This treatment is useful for those with hesitation about committing to a spiritual quest and a desire to surrender to an outside authority, which comes from a need for reassurance. Place the stone between your eyes for 20 minutes, morning and night. Contemplate the garnet. Warning: this stone has energetic effects that can cause you to break off relationships and make irrevocable decisions. Alternate with the methods used for Inner Harmony.

Spiritual Intoxication

Stones: Amethyst, agate, malachite, obsidian

Chakra: Sahasrara chakra (top of the head)

Color: Purple

Instructions: Wear an amethyst jewel. Meditate on an obsidian stone. Drink a glass of agate water morning and night. Drink a glass of amethyst water at noon. Place the malachite on the top of your head for 20 minutes, three times a day.

Strengthening Your Evolutionary Power

Stones: Aventurine, amethyst, chrysocolla, chrysoprase, chrysolite

Chakra: Ajna chakra (brow)

Colors: Blue, purple, gold

Instructions: Place a stone between your eyes twice a day for 20 minutes. Practice active meditation for up to an hour on the night of a full moon. Contemplate the colors.

Zeal

See Intolerance

BOOKS OF RELATED INTEREST

The Seven Archetypal Stones
Their Spiritual Powers and Teachings
by Nicholas Pearson

Crystals for Karmic Healing
Transform Your Future by Releasing Your Past
by Nicholas Pearson
Foreword by Judy Hall

Stone Medicine
A Chinese Medical Guide to Healing with Gems and Minerals
by Leslie J. Franks

Healing Stones for the Vital Organs
83 Crystals with Traditional Chinese Medicine
by Michael Gienger and Wolfgang Maier

Himalayan Salt Crystal Lamps
For Healing, Harmony, and Purification
by Clémence Lefèvre

Shungite
Protection, Healing, and Detoxification
by Regina Martino

The Healing Intelligence of Essential Oils
The Science of Advanced Aromatherapy
by Kurt Schnaubelt, Ph.D.

Vibrational Medicine
The #1 Handbook of Subtle-Energy Therapies
by Richard Gerber, M.D.

Inner Traditions • Bear & Company
P.O. Box 388
Rochester, VT 05767
1-800-246-8648
www.InnerTraditions.com

Or contact your local bookseller